Choosing Your Retirement Hobby

Designed for people who want something constructive and creative to fill their leisure hours, this book offers a wide range of possibilities — from sit-down hobbies like fly-tying and calligraphy to such outdoor activities as tricycling and glassing.

To help the reader make the best choice for his or her abilities, temperament, and budget, the book supplies practical information on cost of materials and tools as well as where to find them; amount of time and work space needed; and the special uses, including charitable ones, to which the hobby can be put. The reader is also directed to books giving detailed instructions for each activity.

Entertaining historical facts about age-old hobbies like origami, plus notes on men and women currently involved in such pursuits as creating bumper stickers and making jigsaw-puzzle table tops, keep the reader amused and interested. There are sections on hobbies for kitchen and workshop, for treasure hunting or sitting quietly; there are nature hobbies, outdoor hobbies, entertainment hobbies; hobbies with crafts, hobbies with living creatures; hobbies new, rediscovered, and offbeat. Intended for

(continued on back flap)

(continued from front flap)

people who are about to or have retired, the book can be of help to anyone interested in taking up something new.

Choosing Your Retirement Hobby

NORAH SMARIDGE

DODD, MEAD & COMPANY · New York

Printed in the United States of America
by Vail-Ballou Press, Inc., Binghamton, N.Y.

Library of Congress Cataloging in Publication Data

Smaridge, Norah.
Choosing your retirement hobby.

Includes bibliographies and index.
1. Aged—Recreation. 2. Hobbies. 3. Handicraft.
4. Retirement. I. Title.
GV184.S62 790.19'26 75-20187
ISBN 0-396-07205-4

For Harriet Holloway

Contents

CHAPTER ONE

Hobbies, New and Rediscovered

MAKING BUMPER STICKERS

An amusing new hobby, especially for those who can turn a lively phrase, is the making of bumper stickers for friends, neighbors, or whomever. With a sticker on his car, any motorist can deliver his message wherever he goes. Nor need he be afraid that people may not read it. According to a *Christian Science Monitor* survey, forty-seven out of fifty drivers read the stickers, even pulling up dangerously close to do so.

No one knows when or where bumper stickers originated, but the Texas Memorial Museum in Austin has a collection of ten thousand, dating back to 1945. The early stickers were either promotional or political, and you could get them free.

Today the printing of bumper stickers is big business. Motorists everywhere apparently jump at the chance to broadcast advice or opinions from the backs of their cars. "Chances are," says columnist Lynde McCormick, "if you have something to say, there's a bumper sticker made to say it." Popular stickers cover law-and-order, ecology, the environment, religion, and music.

But ingenious as they are, bumper-sticker companies can't come up with every message a motorist wants to broadcast. This is where the enterprising hobbyist steps in. He or she can make individual stickers to order, featuring a message supplied by the client, helping him to compose one, or framing something crisp and catchy from his vague idea.

Various types of pressure-sensitive paper can be used to make stickers. And inexpensive kits are available in some hobby shops. There is even a "Bumper Sticker Song," written by country-folk recording artist Larry Grace. In it he refers to "sign-post model Fords" and "rolling billboards out of GMC."

SHIRRET

The brain child of Louise McCrady of West Hartford, Connecticut, shirret is a new technique for producing deep-pile table mats, chair and bench covers, pillows, stair treads, and rugs up to room size. As the name suggests, shirret is a combination of shirring and crochet.

Taught the gentle art of the early shirred rug by her mother, Louise began to concentrate on her own innovations. The simple, updated, economical method which she devised has been hailed as "ecology at its best." Unlike the expensive materials needed for most needlecrafts, shirret makes use of every conceivable kind of fabric leftover—faded dust ruffles, shabby curtains, old or outgrown clothing, threadbare tablecloths and napkins, etc. "So you thought those old blue jeans were ready for the rag pile," said Marilyn Heise, *Chicago Sun-Times* reporter, on discovering shirret. "Not yet. There's a new needlecraft technique which will recycle them, believe it or not, into a rug or pillow which is luxuriously soft and velvety and will last a lifetime."

In making shirret, fabric is cut into strips and then threaded onto a special shirret needle by running the needle in and out through the center of each strip, somewhat like doing a basting stitch in sewing. This forms shirred folds on the needle. These are next attached to the body of the work with crochet stitches of carpet warp. As a stitch of warp is completed, a fold of fabric is slipped off the needles. Thus the fold is held in place between the folds of the preceding row by the stitch of warp. Because the warp stitches are hidden inside the shirred folds, each piece is completely reversible, with beautiful deep pile.

A great variety of fabrics can be used for making shirret—cotton, wool, linen, rayon, knits, corduroy, even bonded and loosely textured fabric. The pieces can be made in any shape, size, color, and in varied textures. This versatility makes it possible for you to make your chair pads, rugs, and other items to fit exactly the size and shape you need, in the colors and designs you want. Thus every piece will be an expression of your own creativity and originality.

The equipment for making shirret is simple and inexpensive. Louise McCrady's book *The Art of Shirret* gives complete and detailed instructions, with diagrams and illustrations, for making each of the basic shapes. It contains patterns for table mats, chair pads and rugs (both in cotton and wool), and directions for a patchwork rug. There are also helpful tips on color planning, and caring for your productions.

The craft requires a special shirret needle. Designed with a long, slender shaft which permits penetration of the fabric, it has a hook at one end, of the correct size for making a crochet stitch of warp. The fingerhold is designed to keep the hook in the working position and prevent the needle from turning in the hand.

The shirret warp, 100 per cent cotton, comes in an 800-yard tube and is sufficient to make four or five chair pads, or a medium-size rug.

Although you can easily learn the technique of shirret from the instruction book, you may like to join a group or class and share your hobby with others. Louise McCrady herself gives programs and demonstrations in many parts of New England. And in New Jersey, Bertha Kleitman, of Morristown, gives courses at the Morris Museum of Arts and Sciences.

Note. A basic kit for shirret making (containing instruction book, shirret needle, and a supply of warp) is priced at $8.50. It can be obtained from Louise McCrady, 30 Rockwell Place, West Hartford, Connecticut 06107. Extra supplies are also available. Helpful extras are a metal gauge for marking fabric strips the correct width (80¢). Marking pins, which look like small safety pins but do not have an extra coil at the end, are helpful as they hang straight in the folds and do not twist or snag the fabric (25¢, pkg. of 10).

DECORATING MAILBOXES

If you live in a township dotted with ugly metal mailboxes, there is a new hobby waiting for you, one dreamed up at approximately the same time by two women living in different parts of the country. In Chesterfield, Virginia, Mrs. John Pierce, running her personal campaign against roadside ugliness, urges neighborhood homeowners to "paint a happy mailbox." She herself has painted more than thirty-six. In Chatham, New Jersey, Mrs. Paul Simpson orders aluminum mailboxes in quantity and decorates them with her own fantasies or with designs suggested by their prospective owners.

Originally, neither hobbyist thought of selling her work. Mrs. Simpson decorated her first box as a wedding gift. Mrs. Pierce painted one to suggest the name of her home, Stoney Grounds, giving it a design of rocks and chipmunks. Her present mailbox has brown thrushes and columbines, the birds and flowers most common in her locality.

Rather to their surprise, the work of both women aroused immediate interest. Gift stores and private customers now buy all they make. "Anyone can do them," Mrs. Pierce says. "You can make them with découpage or use stencils from the dime store." Mrs. Simpson uses an Oriental brush stroke technique, learned during a year in Taiwan.

Mrs. Simpson buys her paint by the quart, and finds that this amount does eighteen mailboxes. If you use latex paint, she warns, you will first have to use a primer to make it adhere to the box. To paint the design, she uses regular artist acrylic tube paints, investing in large tubes for economy. At the present time, her mailboxes sell for from $18.00 to $25.00.

TINSEL PAINTING

If you want an out-of-the-way hobby, and are artistic but not innovative, try resurrecting an old art form. One that gives fascinating results is tinsel painting, a once popular art which dropped out of sight toward the end of the last century. Betty Ely, of Plainfield, New Jersey, came across some samples while browsing in the Metropolitan Museum of Art, and she determined to master the technique. Today she is probably the only exponent of tinsel painting; some of her own pictures hang in the "Met," and her reproductions of "Compote of Fruits and Flowers," by an unknown artist, are sold in the museum's gift shop.

Tinsel painting is done with oils on glass, with aluminum foil as a backdrop to give it glitter. "It is the sparkle that attracts," Mrs. Ely told interviewer Joseph Rush. "There is no other form of art to match it."

A young American girl originated the art during the 1790's when her father, a sea captain, sailed home from China with a picture decorated with mother-of-pearl. The girl was fascinated by its shimmering beauty and pondered how she could get the same effect. She took the tinfoil wrapping from a package of tea, held it behind a piece of colored glass—and was on her way to inventing tinsel painting.

The early tinsel painters, says Mrs. Ely, were "very crude." But as they became more sophisticated, their work was found in many homes. In the days of candlelight, the paintings were especially attractive as they reflected the golden glow of the candle flame.

If you decide to try tinsel painting, you will need sheets of glass, in sizes to suit your subjects; paints; varnish; paintbrushes; aluminum foil. Mrs. Ely finds it easiest to fit her glass into a rack with a light behind it.

Experiment with your oils until you get a consistency that will not run on the glass. "The paints must be clear, with jewel-tone reds and blues," says Mrs. Ely. "Muddiness will destroy the work."

To get diamond-like facets, and to reflect light in varying degrees, crumple and then reshape the foil before fixing it behind the glass and framing your picture.

MAKING YOUR ECOLOGY BOXES

Keep your eyes open in gift shops and you will see eager buyers of "ecology boxes," updated "shadow boxes" containing shells, cones, feathers, seeds, pebbles, and other natural objects. These are highly popular for replacing the more conventional pictures on the living room walls.

An attractive ecology box costs from about $15.00 up. But, like Jerry Canaley, retired banker of North Arlington, New Jersey, you can make your own boxes for $3.00 or $4.00.

Mr. Canaley's hobby keeps him busy and absorbed. "It's something interesting to do," he told interviewer Barbara Kukla, "and it's good therapy. I work at my own pace, an hour here and there in my leisure time."

His new interest also takes him outdoors to treasure hunt. He combs flea markets, garage sales, gift shops, dime stores, looking for miniatures—china teapots, vases, plates—to furnish his boxes and set off the natural objects. From his summer home on a Long Island beach, he scavenges for clamshells and swamp grasses. And, wherever he finds them, he scoops up outdated and out-of-print periodicals. Later, he transforms the illustrations into pictures, framed or unframed, to use in one of the "cubicles" in his ecology boxes.

If you have a modicum of skill in carpentry, you can turn out your own imaginative boxes. Mr. Canaley uses a band saw to cut boxwood into strips for a 6½″ x 12½″ box with nine cubicles. He stains the wood and puts the pieces together with airplane glue, forming compartments of different sizes and shapes against a suitable backing.

He next selects the items to be displayed—perhaps shells, a cluster of bird feathers, some dried berries, and a quaint illustration from the prestigious old *Burr McIntosh Monthly*. For your own boxes, you can gather specimens of the local flora and fauna and add a miniature or two in ceramic, glass, or metal.

Such items as dried flowers should be glued to the box in a natural arrangement. Items like beans and seeds can be left loose in their cubicles. Finally, the front of the box is carefully covered with glass.

ROLLER SKATING

For exercise that is really fun, combined with entertainment and an opportunity to make new friends, try roller skating. Thanks to the nostalgia craze, this favorite of the Gay Nineties has made a comeback all over the country. Nor is it confined to the younger generation; according to *Time*, "gutsy oldsters are invading the rinks, brushing up on fancy footwork learned in the '30's."

Compared with the "skating palaces" of the '30's, which were little more than dingy teen-age hangouts, today's "rollerdromes" are attractive and well run. Behavior on the skating floor is decorous; in most, uniformed guards keep out undesirables.

The rinks are well lighted and climate controlled, and there is music to skate by. "If you are wondering about the attractiveness or safety of your local rink, pay it a visit," advises John J. Schneider, manager of the Livingston, New Jersey, Roller Rink. "Take a good look at the foyer, rest rooms, snack bar, souvenir shop and whatever. If they are well kept and inviting, you can be sure that the skating surface is also well maintained."

Mr. Schneider recommends roller skating as an effective way for retirees and seniors to get the kind of moderate exercise their doctors recommend. "It helps balance and coordination—and it's so simple. It takes only a few lessons, group or private, to get you started off right, and then you can proceed at your own pace to become expert." John Newill, 76, who skates thrice weekly at the Skyline Rink in San Diego, California, sees roller skating as "the finest sport and exercise, and the best muscle-strengthening exercise of all sports." He should know. Besides roller skating and ice skating, he plays tennis six days a week.

One of the things that makes roller skating an appealing hobby is its moderate cost. You can enjoy yourself for a whole evening, as a skater or spectator or both, for less than it costs to see a movie. Admission is between $1.50 and $2.00, plus 75¢ or so for the hire of a pair of skates. If you prefer to own them, you can buy them at the skate store in the rollerdrome, where there is always a good variety, priced to fit any budget. Today's indoor skates are permanently attached to boots, and have wood, fiber, or plastic wheels, which run on precision bearings.

No special outfit is necessary. The right clothes for skating are *comfortable* clothes, loose enough to allow complete freedom of movement. Slacks and sports shirts are fine for men. For women, skirts of a pleated or flared type are effective and are easy to skate in. Slacks, especially those made of stretch materials, are excellent.

While they will scarcely be tempted by the more rugged forms of roller skating (speed skating, skating backward, acrobatic types of figure skating, etc.), senior skaters can, and do, enjoy that most sociable of forms, dance skating with a partner. When proficient, they can enter the contests held from time to time in the rollerdrome. They will be judged on their timing with the music, and on their grace and skill.

The do's and don't's of roller skating and the "house rules" of the rollerdrome are easily learned. In addition, here are a few suggestions which senior skaters would be well advised to follow.

1. See your doctor before you start skating. He can tell you how often, and for how long a period, you should skate. Red Hanley, of Summit, New Jersey, who is teaching his wife to skate, says: "Ten minutes at a time is enough for most seniors, especially if they are beginners. Sit down, relax, and take a good breather before going back on the rink."

2. Before starting, make sure that your skates are properly laced and securely tied. A loose shoelace can foul your wheels and cause a tumble.
3. One at a time, shake each skate. Are there any rattles? Does anything seem loose? If so, investigate and have the trouble corrected; there is usually a skate repair shop in the rollerdrome. A loose wheel or skate assembly can separate from your skate, causing you to fall.
4. Don't try to outdo the younger skaters. Take it easy, as Joseph Oexner, of Mount Dora, Florida, does. Joe, who started roller skating at sixty-eight, has had very few spills. "That's because I don't show off," he says. "And I keep my mind on what I'm doing."

For the location of your nearest roller skating rink, and for booklets and periodicals about skating, write to RSROA (Roller Skating Rinks of America), Box 81846, Lincoln, Nebraska 68510.

For Further Reading

Roller Figure Skating Book, Roller Free Skating Book, Roller Dance Books 1 and *2* (Each, $2.00. Available from RSROA, Box 81846, Lincoln, Neb. 68510)

CHAPTER TWO

Hobbies That Take You Outdoors

TRICYCLING

If you'd like to cycle as a hobby but feel unsafe on a two-wheeler, try a tricycle. These newly sophisticated vehicles are tip-proof, easy to pedal, and equipped for comfort with "Western saddles," padded seats much like those on tractors. If you live in close quarters, or want to take your tricycle along with you on automobile trips, you can get a folding model that takes up a minimum of space.

The cost won't ruin your budget. Prices range from $80.00 to $157.00. Browse through the *Consumer Guide Bicycle Test Reports 14191* ($1.95 from Publications International, 7954 N. Karlov Ave., Skokie, Illinois 60075) before making a choice. It contains an excellent list of adult tricycles, with descriptions and prices. (The latter, of course, are subject to revision.)

Riding a tricycle is one of the most healthful hobbies for seniors. Nationally known heart specialists advise that it is good for the heart, lungs, and muscles. The late Paul Dudley White, cardiologist who treated President Dwight D. Eisenhower, once said: "I'd like to put everybody on bicycles, . . . not once in a while, but regularly, as a routine. It's a good way to prevent heart disease." And a group of Philadelphia physicians, practicing what they preach, have formed a club that enjoys Sunday outings on Fairmount Park's cycling paths. Health and fitness devotees are invited to join them.

Ralph Hanneman, of the Bicycle Institute of America, advises would-be tricyclists to *try* the machine before they buy. "The riding technique is quite different from that used on regular bicycles," he says, "and they are a little harder to pedal. But that minor drawback is made up for in their safety and the fact that people with no ability to balance can master them quickly and easily."

Once you have purchased your trike, proceed warily. Before you venture onto streets, practice riding on your driveway or a quiet path in the park. Concentrate on getting complete control of your machine. Learn to ride straight; weaving and wavering make you a danger to yourself and others.

When you are satisfied with your performance, go farther. Ride on the extreme right, and keep an eye out for potholes. Some cyclists say they feel safer riding on the left, where they can see oncoming traffic. But this practice is frowned upon; in some states it is *illegal* to cycle on the left of the road.

Observe the same rules as the motorist. Stop at all STOP signs and red lights. Slow down and look both ways at intersections. Give hand signals—and make them unmistakable. Don't ride in the wrong direction on a one-way street. Be especially careful about two common dangers—the parked car that may pull out unexpectedly and the car that turns left in front of you.

Tricycling as a hobby will open up new worlds and new interests. When the novelty of riding alone has worn off, you may feel the urge to start a club and organize rides. Write to the League of American Wheelmen (P.O. Box 3928, Torrance, California 90510) for assistance. If you prefer just one or two riding companions, a call to your local recreational department or chamber of commerce will probably provide the name and address of someone in your community interested in riding.

If you want to join an established club, they exist all over the country, from the Anchorage Bike Club in Alaska to the New Orleans Bike Club in Louisiana. Names and addresses are listed in a wonderfully comprehensive booklet, *Bicycle Club Directory and Other Stuff,* put out by the Bicycle Institute of America, Inc. (122 E. 42nd St., New York, N.Y. 10017).

That "other stuff" will give you ideas about cycle-related hobbies you might like to take up. Want to collect bicycle stamps? Write to the Secretary of the Bicycle Stamp Collectors (1457 Cleveland Road, Wooster, Ohio 44691). Or you might make a hobby of visiting antique bike museums, showing bike films at home, or following the exploits of unicyclists and high-wheel riders.

One tricycle hobbyist is helping with the ecology movement. He is designing bike-ecology buttons that urge people to use bikes and trikes more, and automobiles less. If you're interested, you can make your own buttons with the help of *Buttons Say It Better* (available free from Hedwig-Marvic Co., 861 Manhattan Ave., Brooklyn, N.Y. 11222).

For Further Reading

The Bicycle in Life, Love, War, and Literature, by Seamus McGonagle (A.S. Barnes and Co., Inc., Cranbury, N.J., 1968)

The Bicycle Book, by Lillian and Godfrey Frankel (Cornerstone Library, Simon and Schuster, Inc., New York, 1972)

The Best of Bicycling, by Harley M. Leete (Pocket Books, New York, 1972)

The Complete Book of Bicycling, by Eugene A. Sloane (Trident Press, New York, 1970)

GLASSING

A hobby for those with easy access to the seashore, glassing can be done in all seasons but is most productive in fall when heavy surfs pound the shore. It is a simple search for shards, beautiful fragments of glass and pottery, cast up by the waves after their long journey from who-knows-where.

"Glassers are a special kind of beachcomber," says John Ferris, a glasser of note, "men and women of a strange intensity, keen vision and immense patience." Where Coney Island and Atlantic City beachcombers look for money, the glasser's search is for beauty—the rare beauty imparted by the sea to bits of glass.

In general, glassers are loners and go their way in silence. From afar, they look like members of some penitential sect as they plod back and forth, their backs bent, their necks burning in the sunlight.

Glassing is the least expensive of hobbies. You need no tools, nothing but a bag in which to carry home your finds. The pieces will be of all sizes, some as small as a dime. The abrasive action of water and sun gives them a soft opaqueness; they glow, rather than shine. Some glassers ponder the problem of where the fragments came from and what they belonged to in the first place. Some can be identified as shards of smashed bottles, vases, lamps, windshields, Mexican chafing dishes, or Italian Chianti flasks.

There is a fierce rivalry among glassers but the rules, although unwritten, are respected. "Keep to your own part of the beach, don't poach; don't relax. Keep your head down; close your ears to the distracting voice of the sea."

What can you do with the season's finds? Your other

hobbies may provide an answer. Use the fragments in mosaic work or collage. Glue pieces to a mobile; the effect is unexpectedly charming. Attach irregular pieces to driftwood sculpture.

Or simply do as most glassers do. After you have had the fun—and the exercise—of the search, put your shards into a large apothecary jar and set it where your jewel-toned treasures will catch the sun.

SHELL GATHERING AND SHELLCRAFT

In itself, shell gathering is a gentle, fascinating hobby, involving fresh air, mild exercise, and little or no expense. The various coasts of America abound in beautiful shells of all sizes. If you live or summer near a beach, you will be able to find shells at any time, with the best specimens showing up at low tide, or after a storm. Sanibel Island, off the west coast of Florida, has some exceptional shells and is a center for shell buyers from all over the world. Along the chilly coasts of New England a quite different variety is found.

The shell gatherer needs only one simple tool, a spatula or palette knife for detaching shells which cling firmly to rocks. Small cotton bags (plastic is apt to tear) are best for carrying the shells home.

From shell collecting to shellcraft is an almost inevitable step. Few collectors can bear simply to hoard their shells. The urge to *do* something with them is too great. In England, Audrey Cameron and Sylvia Wall pursue the double hobby of shell gathering and shellcraft. They visit beaches all over England, but occasionally run out of supplies; beach pollution is currently causing a shell shortage. When this happens, Audrey and Sylvia buy foreign shells by the pint. Shell dealers everywhere sell shells in bulk for shellcraft as well as special shells for collectors.

The two women wash their finds and grade them according to color—steely blues, shades of pink, bright yellow, and pure white. Then they use them to make pictures, plaques, and shell-encrusted lamps, which "sell like hotcakes" in their hometown of Darlington, Durham. Both women find working with shells a happy change from their daily job of making cattle blood tests for the Ministry of Agriculture.

The necessary materials for shellcraft are easy to come by. You will need tweezers with pointed ends; cotton; transparent glue; toothpicks; bonding cement; a piece of glass or tile large enough to work on; and a razor blade or Exacto knife.

If you are going to use shells which you have gathered yourself, you must first clean them. Boil them for half an hour, and then pick out the meat with tweezers, making sure that the interiors are perfectly clean. Leave the shells to soak overnight in a strong solution of household bleach to remove any lingering fishy odor. Lime deposits can be removed with a diluted solution of muriatic acid. The color of the shells can be preserved, and they can be given an attractive sheen, by rubbing them with oil or spraying them with a plastic preservative spray.

The large, more common shells are easy for the beginner to handle. You can glue several together and fasten them to a plastic base to form a snack dish for the porch or patio table. Candy dishes can be made in the same way. You can also make unusual soapdishes, decorating them with pearls and costume "jewels."

You can use some of your shells in a tray or table top. Arrange a group of shells in a pretty design and glue them onto a sheet of black paper which has previously been fastened to a piece of plywood. Then attach four strips of plywood, each two inches wide, to the bottom piece, to form a shallow box. Finally, cover the entire top with glass to prevent shell breakage. If you want to use the tray as a table top, attach wooden or wrought iron legs to it.

Large shells can form the center of interest when you decorate a plain rattan or wooden handbag. Besides the shells, use jewels, pearls, and any kind of glitter. Leave the handbag in its natural color or spray it with any color paint you wish.

With tiny and small shells, you can make an endless variety of flower pieces, pictures, and fantasies. One way is to drill fine holes into the shells and then thread fine wire through them so that they will hold in whatever arrangement you dream up. Or you can make petals from little cup-shaped shells and choose others whose shapes are suitable for leaves and stems. Work on a piece of glass and begin by putting a small spot of glue or cement, about the size of the flower you wish to make, on the glass. Work from the outside of the flower toward the center, using tweezers to put the shell petals into the proper arrangement. Hobby stores have booklets with step-by-step instructions for making many kinds of shell flowers.

Shells can be used to decorate one-of-a-kind wastebaskets, tissue holders, powder boxes, and other items. For the shell-flower centers, use rhinestones or tiny pearls. Lacquer or paint the shells, or spray pearl lacquer onto the flower arrangement to give it a pearl glow. Shellcraft designs and flowers can also be used on tally cards and place cards.

For Further Reading

Art from Shells, by Stuart and Leni Goodman (Crown Publishers, Inc., New York, 1972)

Shellcraft Instruction, by Marjorie and Frank Pelosi (Great Outdoors Publishing Co., St. Petersburg, Fla.)

The Shell Collector's Handbook, by A. Hyatt Verrill (G.P. Putnam's Sons, New York, 1950)

A Field Guide to the Shells of Our Atlantic and Gulf Coasts, by Percy Morris (Houghton Mifflin Co., Boston, 1952)

MAKING RUBBINGS

When they wrote their recent *Memorials for Children of Change: The Art of Early New England Stone Carving,*

Dickran and Ann Tashjian relied largely on rubbings for illustration. Artistic, softly dark, the rubbings were particularly appropriate in a book about gravestones, memorials which have inspired some of the best rubbings made by hobbyists.

A modern revival of an ancient art, making rubbings is the technique of reproducing the handsome, intricate, or amusing designs and inscriptions found on brass, stone, or other types of commemorative objects. The hobby started in our country in 1886, when the Monumental Brass Society was founded. This national organization was aimed at studying and preserving brasses. The members first made rubbings as a record of existing brasses but the purpose was soon forgotten and making rubbings became simply an unusual and delightful pastime.

No special talent is needed for brass or stone rubbing, and the necessary materials, paper and rubbing wax or chalk, are inexpensive. For advance practice, use a pad of cheap newsprint. As soon as you have learned the knack of rubbing—and it does not take long—switch to a better grade of paper. Rice paper is excellent, but expensive. Architect's tracing paper, available in drafting supply stores, works well and has the advantage of coming in rolls in a good range of widths. For most rubbings, the 24″ width is practical; it is priced at from $3.50 to $5.00 a roll. Easiest to use is Aqaba paper, developed by Oldstone Enterprises, 66 Summer St., Boston, Massachusetts 02110. This has multidirectional strength and has been specially treated so that it is usable even under damp conditions. A 24″ x 36″ sheet costs 40¢, postpaid. It is also available in rolls 40″ wide, at 65¢ a yard, postpaid.

You can use wax crayons for your rubbings but avoid those that are too greasy; they give uneven build-up. Litho-sticks, large, soft wax crayons, are good. They cost $1.50 each and are available from Arthur Brown and Bro., Inc., 2 West 46th St., New York, N.Y. 10036. An excellent wax is Oldstone's Rubbing Wax, a hard wax with a high melting point that makes a good, even impression. A quarter-pound cupcake costs $2.00, postpaid.

When making a rubbing, attach the paper firmly to the object from which you want to make it. Then rub the design or lettering carefully and smoothly with your wax or chalk, keeping the pressure even. The raised portion of the design will be picked up, leaving the depressed parts white. It is as simple as that.

Hobbyists keep rolls of paper, plus chalk or wax, in their cars or bicycle baskets, so that they will be prepared whenever they happen upon an interesting stone or brass object with a good design or inscription. Some hobbyists point with pride to rubbings as long as five feet. These they turn into beautiful wall hangings.

Where shall you look for objects? There are thousands of examples in all countries, brass and stone memorials which have survived wars, vandals, and the ravages of weather. A current advertisement offers Chinese stone rubbings "executed on heavy rice paper, of the Han and later dynasties." Memorial brasses were first produced in Germany and Belgium in medieval days. They were usually rectangular sheets of metal, on which the portrait of the deceased was represented, usually up to life size, by deeply incised lines, often filled with an enamel-like substance. In England, where brass was less plentiful, the figure was usually cut out of the metal and inserted in stone or marble slabs.

If you wish, you can confine your rubbings to those which illustrate a single theme—for instance, the evolution of fashion. Brasses depicting women show the changing fashions in dress and hair styles. Rubbings showing the various types of ecclesiastical dress also make a good collection. Military uniforms, too, often appear on brasses. In England, knights were sometimes shown in their armor. Borders with decorative figures of angels and saints were common, and many of the inscriptions were executed in beautiful lettering.

You need not, however, go far afield to pursue your hobby. Start in your own locality. You will find interesting inscriptions on the plaques that mark historic houses, buildings, and old mills. In Upper Montclair, New Jersey, on a small stone outside his early home, an inscription commemorates astronaut Buzz Aldrin. Your local historical society will be able to tell you the location of stones in your area which commemorate battles, historic events, visits of famous personages, and the like.

Permission to make rubbings on private property is invariably granted pleasantly; and the owner, appreciative of your interest, may fill in historical details for you. Ask permission of the superintendent or caretaker before you venture into cemeteries or churchyards to make rubbings of tombstone inscriptions.

Don't be surprised if you gather a little crowd of spectators. People like to watch this work. Answer their questions; in return, ask them to direct you to markers and plaques in their own neighborhoods.

Although a recent revival, the hobby of making brass or stone rubbings is rapidly widening in scope. "It's like stamp collecting, or collecting coins," says one hobbyist. "People collect rubbings and form clubs to study, trade, and discuss them. Certain rubbings are naturally more important than others from both the artistic and historic point of view."

For Further Reading

The Last Word, by Dr. M. Williams (Oldstone Enterprises, Boston, Mass., 1973)

Memorials for Children of Change, by Dickran and Ann Tashjian (Wesleyan University Press, Middletown, Conn., 1974)

Stories Behind the Stones, by Gail M. Potter (A.S. Barnes and Co., Inc., Cranbury, N.J., 1969)

ARCHERY

Do you fancy a hobby that goes back to the Stone Age? Archery is the answer. Very early writings indicate that archery has always been practiced for fun as well as in warfare. The foremost archers of antiquity were the Egyptians, who used bows a little shorter than a man, and arrows, headed with bronze or flint, two to three feet long. On the authority of the Bible and other writings, the Jews were deadly with a bow made of reed, wood, or horn.

At some time in their history, civilized people all over the world have made use of the bow. In our own country, archery began in 1828, when a group of young men founded a club known as the United Bowmen of Philadelphia. Today there are many archery clubs throughout the country, and the hobbyist does not have to look far for a group to join. At American universities, archery is usually a part of physical training—highly popular with girls because it is wonderful for the figure.

Select your bow to suit your strength and ability. The beginner's bow should be made of lemonwood, and the wood must be thoroughly seasoned; tests have shown that the presence of moisture in unseasoned wood lowers its strength considerably.

The arrows can also be made of wood, but modern archers are experimenting with such materials as tubular steel, aluminum, Duralumin, and bamboo.

To do well at archery, and to win matches, the technique must be mastered. Join a class if you can. If not, begin the study of archery in the right way, because if you start haphazardly it will take long, hard work to overcome sloppy habits. Phillip Rounsevelle's *Archery Simplified* will not only teach you the correct principles but will tell you how to teach others—a consideration if you are the type who inspires friends and neighbors.

Is archery dangerous? Not if sensible precautions are taken. The archer should never point a drawn bow and arrow toward a person. Accidents on the range are always due to someone's stupidity. Show-offs should stay at home—or keep remembering that bows and arrows have been used as weapons for thousands of years!

Unless you have plenty of acreage, don't try to shoot in your backyard. If you live near open fields, however, you can improvise a range very easily. If you are a town dweller, you can become affiliated with a club and shoot under supervision, often in the local armory. In either case, archery is a year-round hobby—and once you have fallen under its spell, it will hold you for years.

For Further Reading

Archery Handbook, by Edmund H. Burke (Arco Publishing Co., New York, 1954)

Archery: The Modern Approach, by Ernest Heath (Landau Book Co., New York, 1966)

KITE FLYING

According to a breezy editorial in the *Hartford Courant,* "Kite flying is for the pure in heart, whose spirits must fly up into the wild blue yonder." Certainly it is a fascinating and healthful hobby, which gets its devotees out into the fresh air and prods them into exercise, gentle or more strenuous according to the whim of the wind and the strength of the kite.

Kite flying is also an inexpensive hobby. Kites that will stand up to a season's use can be had for $5.00 up, although you can pay as much as $45.00 for an exquisite, handpainted Indian kite. It is also comparatively simple to make your own kite, or assemble one from a kit. In a single summer, Tomi Ungerer, who writes and illustrates his own books, completed more than one hundred flying kites, of all sizes and shapes and with acrylic painted designs.

Anything with a shape that gives "lift" in a breeze but remains tethered to the ground qualifies as a kite. The variety of shapes seems to be endless. Favorite of beginning flyers is the classic "two sticker," of roughly diamond shape and carrying a tail for balance. Commonly seen, too, are the rectangular box kites which have long been used by the military and in meteorology. Perhaps the most familiar model seen in parks and on beaches is the triangular-shaped "Coyne," a French military kite.

Easiest to transport is the newly designed "sled" kite, so called because it resembles a snowsled. As it has no lateral stiffening, it can be rolled up and carried in a tube. "Delta wing" kites are also easy to carry. They have wide, triangular-shaped flying surfaces, usually of cloth or plastic.

Experts vote for the "parawings," distant relatives of parachutes, and almost indestructible. Their basic feature is a central crease; all other elements are free to flop.

Perhaps the most exciting to fly are the new "Jalnert parafoils" that look like billowing air mattresses tugging at the wind.

But for everyday flying, says Will Yolen (who once broke the record by flying 178 kites on a single line), any kite will do. You can fly it on a beach, in a meadow, or in the public park, but make sure that you are on the right side of the law. At the turn of the century, when electric and telephone wires began to spread across the continent, many cities and towns passed a law stating that "it shall not be lawful for any person or persons to set up or fly any kite . . . in or upon or over any street, avenue, alley or open space, public enclosure or square within the limits of the city." That law is still on many books, although seldom enforced, but kite flyers are attacking it vigorously.

When you go off to fly your kite, take note of the wind velocity. You will need at least a four-mile-an-hour wind. "If you see smoke moving out and away from a chimney," says Will Yolen, "you have enough wind to fly a light kite without a tail. If the wind is more than ten miles an hour—when flags are flapping in the breeze—you'd better attach a tail."

As soon as the wind takes hold of the kite, begin to let out line immediately. Do not run with the wind; run against it, letting out line as you go.

Instead of running, you can cast your kite into the wind on an old fishing rod and reel. Sweep the rod over your head, and let out line easily at first until the wind takes it firmly. Then let the reel run free, checked only by your thumb as a drag. Do not use the drag on the reel because it does not have the sensitivity of your thumb.

Never attempt to fly your kite in the rain, or during an electrical storm. You probably know about Benjamin Franklin's kite-and-key experiment with lightning. In that case, a kite helped to prove that lightning and electricity are the same. However, Ben took a highly dangerous risk; had lightning struck that brass key, he could easily have been electrocuted.

Finally, keep your kite away from power lines and the vicinity of an airport.

"Just get the kite up," advises Will Yolen, "and you will find other 'brothers in the sky.' " Kite flying, according to him, is a sociable hobby, and one that certainly beats dog walking for meeting interesting people.

For Further Reading

Flying Kites: In Fun, Art, and War, by James Wagenvoord (The Macmillan Co., New York, 1968)

The Young Sportsman's Guide to Kite-Flying, by Will Yolen (Thomas Nelson and Sons, Ltd., London, 1963)

Chinese Kites: How to Make Them and Fly Them, by David F. Jue (C. E. Tuttle Co., Inc., Rutland, Vermont, 1967)

World on a String, by Jane Yolen (World Publishing Company, New York, 1969)

CHAPTER THREE

Workshop Hobbies

MAKING JIGSAW TABLE TOPS

To many adults, solving jigsaw puzzles is a hobby in itself. The results are gratifying, especially when the puzzle is a reproduction of Fragonard's "Blind Man's Buff," Gauguin's "Waterlilies," or some other masterpiece.

Retired executive George Payne, of Springfield, New Jersey, solved a number of puzzles while recuperating from an illness. His wife suggested that he make a table top out of one of the finished puzzles—a glowing beauty with a design of tawny chrysanthemums. He did, and the table is a decorative note in their living room.

If you enjoy working with wood and the gluepot, you can transform your own and your friends' completed puzzles into end tables, cocktail tables, and trays.

Or, like Mr. Payne, you can make them to order. His invitation brings results:

> You choose your puzzle, and have all the fun
> Of finding the pieces, one by one,
> Put them together as soon as you're able.
> Then I'll get busy and make you a table.

Be discriminating about the puzzles you work with. Small, cheap puzzles with less than a hundred pieces are not worth your time. Select Eaton or Springbok or other fine quality puzzles, with from 500 to 650 pieces. There is a huge variety of subjects to choose from—maps, reproductions of decorative art, pets, ecological themes, and so on.

You will need ½″ plywood; rails, 1½″ high; molding; paint; varnish; and a bottle of Puzzle-Saver Preservative (obtainable in hobby shops). Table legs can be bought ready made.

Give the puzzle a coating of the puzzle-saver, a transparent glue which holds the pieces together. Then cut your plywood to the exact shape of the puzzle. "Octagonal and round puzzles are prettier than square," Mr. Payne notes. "Oblong has the disadvantage that the picture is on the vertical, and if it is a coffee table it is lost to the view of those sitting on the sofa."

Choose the molding and table legs carefully so that their form and color will be appropriate for the puzzle picture. For instance, Mr. Payne used a twisted rope type of molding to frame a puzzle of a whaling ship.

Glue the puzzle to the plywood, and glue the molding in place around the edge. Then give puzzle and molding four coats of clear varnish to seal out moisture.

Smaller finished puzzles, if worth keeping, can be affixed to a cork base and used for wall decor. Sandy Miller's charming little *Thingies,* circular puzzles with fantastic designs, lend themselves beautifully to this method of finishing.

WATCH AND CLOCK REPAIRING

Although there are books to consult and catalogs that list thousands of clock and watch parts, repairing is not necessarily a textbook hobby. If you wish, you can join the many clock repairers who are self-taught. You will need good eyesight, some mechanical skill, the ability to use small tools—and plenty of patience.

You also need a quiet temperament. In general, the clock repairer is a loner; he enjoys working by himself and at his own pace. Later, when he has gained experience, he may want to get in touch with other hobbyists. He can then join the National Association of Watch and Clock Collectors and find out from them the names of people in his community who are interested in clocks and their mechanisms.

You will need a number of old clocks and watches to work on, preferably expendable. Your own household, and friends and neighbors, can probably furnish all you need. Flea markets, garage sales, and the like will also turn up old clocks at low prices.

The necessary tools include a screwdriver, a pair of flat pliers, a pair of pinch-nose pliers, a small paint-brush, benzine for cleaning the parts, and clock oil for lubricating. Essentials are a good light, and a loupe, or magnifying lens, such as jewelers wear.

You can work at a desk or a medium-sized, sturdy table. Have at hand a stack of the small, transparent envelopes used by stamp collectors. These will hold the tiny screws and delicate parts which can so easily get mislaid or omitted.

The mechanism of a clock may look complicated, but it is actually simpler than most pieces of machinery. The working principle of various types of clocks is the same; once you have discovered it, you will find it relatively easy to set about making repairs.

Benjamin Banneker, in the eighteenth century, managed to make a clock without ever having seen one. His schoolmaster gave him a picture of a clock which he found in an English magazine. He also supplied him with books on motion and geometry. With these aids, plus a borrowed watch, Benjamin set to work.

He first took the watch to pieces, spread the cogs and wheels in front of him, and painstakingly reassembled them. He repeated the process until he knew precisely how the parts fitted together. That done, he began his clock-making project, using his only tool, a penknife. Lacking the means to cut metal into intricate shapes, he carved the clock parts out of wood. The one exception was the metal he used for the striking system.

It took Ben two years to finish his clock to his satisfaction. It was a stunning achievement. People came from all around to see the wooden timepiece which kept accurate time and chimed on the hour.

More fortunate than Ben, you yourself can start practicing on a clock rather than a watch. Practice dissembling and reassembling it until you find out "what makes it tick." Often, when you have removed the mechanism carefully from the case and cleaned and oiled it, you will find that you can start the clock again. Dust and grime clogging the works are responsible for most cases of stoppage. If you find that this is not the cause, you will need to examine every part, consulting a repair manual if the trouble does not come to light. If the mechanism is unusual, you can usually get help and advice from your local clock collectors' club. Information is also at hand in collectors' magazines and bulletins.

You can extend your hobby pleasurably by browsing around in flea markets, garage sales, secondhand stores, and the like, looking for interesting old clocks which can be repaired and sold to collectors, interior decorators, and others.

For information, inspiration, and general interest read some of the many beautiful books on clock history. *Clocks,* by Simon Fleet, is especially delightful; it deals with domestic clocks from the end of the fourteenth century to the present day. The illustrations include much that is of interest to clock repairers, including many diagrams of clock mechanisms.

FOR FURTHER READING

Watch and Clock Making and Repair, by W. J. Gazeley (Transatlantic Arts, Inc., Levittown, N.Y., 1974)

Modern Course in Watch and Clock Repairing, by P. Buford Harris (Nelson-Hall Co., Chicago, 1944)

The Book of American Clocks, by Brooks Palmer (The Macmillan Co., New York, 1950)

Handbook of Watch and Clock Repairs, by H. G. Harris (Emerson Books, Inc., New York, 1974)

ANTIQUING

If you are handy with a paintbrush and have a flair for design, you will find antiquing an amusing and profitable hobby. It is the art of refinishing by applying American antique decoration. The crafts used are simple but take time, enthusiasm, and perseverance.

Almost anything can be antiqued, including furniture, so long as the object has pleasing lines, and is intact. It does not matter if it is chipped or cracked; indeed, chips and cracks help the "antique" effect. Some hobbyists choose to work on objects of intrinsic value, like chairs, footstools, library stepstools. Others make something out of nothing by beautifying items which have been dismissed as junk. Dough and salt boxes, butter tubs, old flatirons (which make eye-catching bookends and doorstops) and coal scuttles lend themselves beautifully to decoration with folk designs.

You will need a well-ventilated working space where you can make a mess with impunity; a basement or garage where there is no dust or damp is ideal. Some of the materials used, like paint or varnish remover, leave strong and unpleasant odors, so keep a window open. Get together plenty of old rags, some paint-brushes in different sizes, fine and coarse sandpaper, steel wool, and whatever you intend to use in the way of paints and varnishes.

If the object is already covered with old paint or varnish, you will need to bare the wood with a good remover and wash and dry it thoroughly. If it is not necessary to remove the old finish, be sure that all wax and grease spots are removed, and fill all the cracks with a wood filler. Smooth the surface and edges with fine sandpaper until all scratches are removed.

There are several types of decoration which can be used successfully. For "country painting," first give the object a coat of flat paint. Then decorate it with an early American folk design, and rub the paint with colored glaze. Finish with a coat of satin varnish to seal and protect the surface.

In freehand bronze painting, use fine bronze powder in shades of gold, copper, or silver, mixed with clear finish lacquer or varnish.

Stenciling is a more tricky type of decoration. This process, with which the makers of Hitchcock-type chairs, Boston rockers, and tinware decorated their products, was kept secret for a hundred years.

The object to be stenciled must be carefully prepared. If it is made of wood, paint it with flat black paint. When thoroughly dry, give it a coat of varnish. The stencil, a design traced on architect's linen and cut out with sharp-pointed scissors, must be put on while the varnish is still sticky. Choose whichever bronze powder you wish and use your finger, wrapped in a piece of silk, as a paintbrush. Rub the powder over the varnished areas exposed by the cuts in the design. If metal is to be stenciled, paint it with a metal primer before applying the flat black paint and varnish.

"Floating color," a very effective type of decoration, is a method of using transparent colors, floated in a mixture of linseed oil and varnish, over opaque colors.

Any of the foregoing decorative methods can be used successfully to antique such things as wastebaskets, mirror frames, barrels, bread boxes, trunks, etc. You can hunt up appropriate and colorful designs at the public library, which will have books on Colonial, Pennsylvania Dutch, and other forms of folk art. Marguerite Ickis' and Reba Esh's *Folk Arts and Crafts* has an excellent chapter on design and color which will suggest many motifs. It is a good idea to assemble your own scrapbook of designs, including clippings from magazines, wallpaper samples, greeting cards, book bindings, and bits of patterned fabrics.

Because a little help and encouragement never come amiss, you could take a few lessons in freehand decorating at the "Y," or in an adult education class. But before you start taking instructions, get some idea of this wide field by reading a few of the many good books and pamphlets on the subject. One which will amuse as well as instruct you is Elizabeth L. Browning's *With Love and Elbow Grease,* which tells competently and entertainingly of her experience in antiquing.

For Further Reading

Tole Painting, by B. K. Fraser (Sterling Publishing Co., Inc., New York, 1971)

The Do-It-Yourself Guide to Restoring Antiques, by Rosemary Ratcliff (Universal Publishing and Distributing Corp., New York, 1974)

Early American Decorating Techniques, by Mariette P. Slayton (The Macmillan Co., New York, 1972)

Decorating Furniture with a Little Bit of Class, by George Grotz (Doubleday and Co., Inc., New York, 1969)

KITE MAKING AND DECORATING

If one of your hobbies is kite flying you can, if you wish, buy all the kites you want. But according to one enthusiast: "There is something about building and flying your own kite that gets into the blood. The project carries you through planning, construction and control. You are architect, contractor, and pilot in rapid succession."

Start by building a classic two-sticker. As you become more experienced, you can proceed to the other basic shapes—the Eddy kite, the stub-nose kite, the Japanese rectangular kite, and others, which will serve as a basis for your own variations. The only equipment you need consists of a ruler or tape measure, strong, light-weight glue, nails, string, scissors or cutting blade, sticks, and covering material. "There are no rules for kite-building," says author James Wagenvoord. "The only requirement is a desire to build something that flies."

In making your first kite, the dimensions are not too important, but the vertical mast must be a little longer than the horizontal spar. Center the spar about one quarter down the mast. Bind them securely in a cross with string.

Notch the stick ends and, if you wish, bind them for reinforcement. Then attach string around the outline of the kite, just tightly enough so the sticks do not buckle.

Tape the frame to your covering material—newspaper, wrapping paper, plastic, or whatever you want to use. Draw an outline of the kite an inch or two larger than the frame. Cut it out, notching it at the corners. Fold it over the string and glue it down firmly.

Make two small holes in the covering, one just to the upper right of the cross joint, the other just to the lower left. Strengthen the surrounding material with the type of linen and glue reinforcing rings used in loose-leaf notebooks. Stick the flying line in one hole and out the other, and tie securely.

Your two-sticker will need a tail. Make holes on either side of the bottom of the mast and reinforce them.

Attach the tail through them. It does not need to be too heavy; try light strips of rag, or use kite line with paper bows every foot or so.

When you wish to try making more sophisticated kites, you will find many books that will give you clear, detailed instructions. One of the best is James Wagenvoord's *Flying Kites: In Fun, Art, and War.*

Decorating kites, whether for flying or not, can be more fascinating than building them. Hobbyists with even a modest talent for designing and painting will find kite decorating an unusual and delightful hobby. Inexpensive paper or fabric kites can be used, with designs painted in acrylic paint. America can point to many successful kite painters, but Japanese artists, both here and in Japan, are producing the most exquisite and authentic kite art. Fumio Yoshimura, who lives and works in the United States, is a kite "sculptor" of rare talent. His kite creations, shaped like moths, fish, and the most delicate birds and insects, are not only beautiful but can be flown. Fumio calls his kites "nonsense art" but warns amateur kite painters that such art must be approached seriously; imaginatively handled, it provides a rich source of ideas for more conventional painting and sculpture.

Today there is a trend toward "kites without wind," kites designed for decorating interiors and not for flying. During the 1960's, "pop" artists discovered the wonderfully decorative quality of kites. Al Hansen, an experimental art instructor at Rutgers University, in New Jersey, bought a dozen two-stick kites to use as wall hangings in his studio. When they were in place, he was impressed by the charm and effectiveness of two of the kites, which were decorated with flags. On impulse, he stretched some large pieces of canvas into kite shapes and began to paint them with "pop" subjects—comic-strip characters and the like. His kite art was well received even by the most serious art critics, and today Hansen's kite paintings are found in private collections and even in some museums.

You can paint your kite with any design you fancy, but make sure that it is bold enough to be effective from a distance. You can tie-dye the fabric as a change from painting. Or, if you wish simply to choose your colors and add finishing touches to a kite to make it an "original," you can buy kits that can be used to complete a paper kite. These kits include crepe-paper kite tails, colored string, decorative adhesive tape, and other materials.

For Further Reading

Kites, by H. Waller Fowler, Jr. (The Ronald Press Co., New York, 1965)

25 Kites That Fly, by Leslie L. Hunt (Dover Publications, Inc., New York, 1971)

Your Book of Kites, by Clive Hart (Transatlantic Arts, Inc., Levittown, New York, 1964)

CHAPTER FOUR

Hobbies for the Kitchen

DECORATING WINDOW SHADES

A hobby with quick and exciting results, this can conveniently be followed in the kitchen because the shades have to be spread on a table or the bare floor. Although the hobby itself is a new one, eye-filling shades have a long history and some are museum pieces.

In the United States, the popularity of painted window shades began in the eighteenth century. The earliest had pastoral scenes of pioneer life. Later ones copied European models and showed stylized mountains and trees, with rivers flowing past melancholy ruined castles.

During the nineteenth century, the artist Pierre Auguste Renoir made his living in Paris by painting shades for the missionaries in the Far East. The shades substituted for stained-glass windows in the primitive chapels, but Renoir was permitted to choose his own subjects, provided they were edifying. "My father had a very good time of it," his son wrote later. " 'I had a trick,' he told me, with a wink. 'I did lots of clouds. You see, a cloud can be daubed on with a few brush strokes.' "

You don't have to be a Renoir to come up with attractive shades. Nor do you need a big investment in supplies. You can begin with inexpensive, ready-made cloth shades, obtainable in dime stores, and use whichever decorating method appeals to you. You can start from scratch and paint, stencil, or appliqué simple designs onto the cloth. Or you can use one of the available do-it-yourself laminations to give your shade an allover pattern. Lam-Eze, and other specially prepared shades to which you can apply your own decorator fabrics, come in kits with easy-to-follow instructions. You can also dress up plain shades with press-on fringes, braid, ribbons, etc.

Painted shades strike a fresh decorative note, and it takes very little artistic talent to do them, freehand, in simple designs which will tie in with the decor of the room and repeat the color points made elsewhere. You can work in any style that appeals to you, traditional or contemporary. Use room-darkening shades for painting because light filtering through the translucent type may show up any uneven application of color. Fine-textured shades will "take" paint more smoothly than coarse ones. Painting works well on most cloth-based shades, but never paint on plastic; the paint may destroy that kind of shade.

Many hobbyists prefer to make bold geometric designs, such as stripes or chevrons. For these, acrylic or vinyl-based wall paints work best. Use the masking tape that is specially made for painting, and apply it to the edges of the area to be painted; this will ensure absolutely straight lines. To make certain that shade, paint, and masking tape are compatible, make a preliminary test on a sample or scrap of the shade cloth. If none is available, unroll the shade all the way down and use an inch or so at the very top, the part that will ordinarily stay wrapped around the roller.

For a lean, contemporary effect, try stencils, either creating your own designs or using the standard type offered in art supply stores. Lay the shade flat, lightly mark in the location of the motifs, and then tape the stencil in place. Use textile paint and a stiff stencil brush. Dip the brush, remove the excess, and work from edge to center until the design is filled in. Don't remove the pattern until the shade is dry. Then clean the stencil and repeat the pattern. After twenty-four hours, apply an iron at low heat for about six minutes, using a press cloth between for protection.

A striking "collage" effect can be achieved with appliqué. Cut motifs from fabric or wall covering and paste them onto plain cloth shades. You can also use decals and flexible "stick-ons," but these will give a more limited choice. Closely woven materials—polished cotton, chintz, percale, felt—are best to use. To keep the fabric from fraying, paint the raw edge of the motifs with colorless nail polish before cutting.

(Felt and wall covering, of course, will not fray.)

Cut out the motifs carefully with small, sharp scissors and arrange them to make a design on the shade. Then apply glue to the reverse side, one motif at a time, making sure that the entire surface is covered before pressing into place. Smooth carefully, checking to see that all the edges are firmly attached and no air bubbles remain. If using sheer fabric, spread the glue directly onto the shade cloth. Always use an adhesive that stays flexible when dry so that the shade can be rolled up when necessary. A good glue for the purpose is Bond Cement No. 693.

If you mistrust your artistic taste or want to do a quick job, fall back on commercial trimmings; the huge variety offered will suggest dozens of lively ways to add color to plain shades. Classic trimmings include loop-edged, tasseled, ball and brush fringes, ribbons, eyelet edging, rickrack, printed borders. Self-adhesive press-on fringes and plastic or fabric tapes make it easy to achieve a custom effect in very little time.

Decide exactly where you want to place the trimming on the shade. It is best to keep it fairly close to the bottom, in the area not ordinarily rolled up. Plan the number of rows and decide whether they are to touch, overlap, or be separated. Use the hemline as a guide in keeping the rows straight, or draw a light pencil line. When applying, do not stretch the trimming taut or it will spring back when the pressure is removed.

As a change from making shades for daily use, turn to seasonal shades that will create a big and original holiday effect. When the festive season is over, they can be rolled up and stored until the following year. Or you can make holiday shades to sell or give; they are a very acceptable item for bazaars and charity sales. It will be best to display samples only, because you will have to measure the windows for which the shades are wanted.

For Halloween, you might make a montage of pumpkins and jack-o'-lanterns; for Christmas, a geometric appliqué angel, or a design of Christmas trees or Santa Clauses. Valentine's Day, Easter, Mothers' Day, and other feast days will suggest happy ideas. And shades decorated with animals, flowers, toys, or objects representing a child's special interests will make charming and unusual gifts for birthdays and other occasions.

For Further Reading

Do-It-Yourself Ideas for Window Shades and *The Decorative Window Shade,* each 25¢, are available from Window Shade Manufacturers Association, Dept. N.S., 230 Park Ave., New York, N.Y. 10017. Leaflets on how to laminate shades are available free from the same address.

Shades of History, by Ruth Lee (Booklet, 25¢. Joanna Western Mills Co., 2141 S. Jefferson St., Chicago, Ill. 60616, 1969)

WINEMAKING

For hours of happy occupation, and a delightful end product, try winemaking. Your hobby can be as simple or as elaborate as you like. In a comparatively short time, even the beginner can build up a modest cellar, enjoy wine with his meals, and have something palatable on hand to offer to his friends.

Equipment will cost you little; most of the things you require for winemaking are at hand in your own kitchen. Essential items are:

One 2-gallon white polythene bucket
A large saucepan
A 1-gallon glass jar
6 feet of ¼″ bore plastic tubing
Polythene sieve
Airlock and bored cork to fit the neck of a gallon jar
(Later) Wine bottles and corks for your finished wine

All the items are made of glass or plastic, for a good reason. Except for stainless steel, fermenting wine should never be in contact with metal objects. Use an oak rod, or a plastic or stainless steel spoon when you stir your wine.

Keep your equipment spotlessly clean. The easiest way to do this is first to wash the items in hot water and then rinse them with a sterilizing solution.

The range of ingredients for winemaking is very wide. If you have a garden or have access to the country, you can gather your raw materials yourself. The fruits chosen must be sound, ripe, clean, and dry.

Although wines can be made from fermented sweetened extract derived from flowers, leaves, and roots, fruit or fruit juice is generally preferred for winemaking by the beginner. The fruit can be fresh, canned, or dried. Whether you use canned fruit in chunks, puree, slices or pieces, they will all make palatable wine.

Dried fruits of all kinds can be used, among them figs, dates, elderberries, bananas, apples, and apricots. For balance, a little citric acid or tannin must be added to fruits which are deficient in them.

"The true winemaker is the yeast," says Cyril Berry, author of *Amateur Winemakers' Recipes*. "We merely put the ingredients together, provide the correct temperature, and leave the yeast to do its work." Wine yeast is preferable to baker's yeast and can be had in dozens of varieties in liquid, dried granules, or tablet form. Some yeast compounds include nutrient chemicals which get fermentation off to a quick start.

To produce healthy, vigorous fermentation, yeast needs certain chemicals. These "yeast nutrients" can be purchased in tablet or powder form. One tablet, or half a teaspoon of powder, is sufficient for a gallon of wine.

Ordinary white granulated sugar gives excellent results. If you want your wine to be dry, do not exceed 2½ pounds of sugar in a gallon. For medium-sweet wines add 2½ to 3 pounds of sugar, and for really sweet wines, use 3½ pounds.

Canned fruits, or even canned orange juice, make delicious wines. Here is Cyril Berry's recipe for a beginner's wine made with orange juice. The same steps can be used in making wines with fresh fruits, canned fruits, or berries.

INGREDIENTS

1 pint can unsweetened orange juice
2½ pounds of sugar
½ teaspoon of dried wine tannin
1 tablet or ½ teaspoon powdered wine yeast
1 nutrient tablet
Water to one gallon

METHOD

Pour the juice into a gallon jar. Dissolve sugar in five pints of boiling water and allow to cool before pouring it into the jar. Add tannin, yeast, and nutrient. Fit the fermentation lock to prevent entry of air or spoilage organism which could cause undesirable flavors. (The airlock also helps the yeast to produce more alcohol.)

Cover the jar with a lid or a piece of polythene sheet, held in place with rubber bands, and leave to ferment. Stir twice daily for a week, and then strain through the polythene sieve into a gallon jar. Pour in cold water to reach the neck of the jar. Fit airlock and cork, and leave the jar in a warm place to finish fermenting.

After eight to ten weeks, fermentation should have ceased. Now siphon the wine into a clean jar; this removes the wine from the yeast and fruit deposit which forms at the bottom of the original jar. If wine stands too long on this sediment, it may spoil.

Leave the wine in the jar for about twelve weeks before you bottle it; this gives it time to clear. Then siphon the wine into clean, sterilized bottles and cork them with either straight-sided corks or flanged corks from your winemaking supplies store.

Unlike most other homemade wines, this beginner's wine will be drinkable within a few months of making. Once you have enjoyed your own product, you will want to try more sophisticated wines, following instructions in some of the excellent winemaking books on the market.

For Further Reading

First Steps in Winemaking, by C.J. Berry (British Book Centre, Inc., New York, 1973)

Winemaking with Concentrates, by Peter Duncan (British Book Centre, Inc., New York, 1974)

Home Winemaker's Handbook, by Walter S. Taylor and R.P. Vine (Harper and Row, Publishers, New York, 1968)

Winemaking with Canned and Dried Fruit, by C.J. Berry (British Book Centre, Inc., New York, 1973)

CANDLEMAKING

Candlemaking, which includes those plump little night lights so reassuring to children and invalids, is today a popular and profitable hobby, thanks to such sophisticated touches as the addition of perfumes and decorations.

Candles have come a long way. Modern candles are the successors of the early rushlights, made from the pith of rushes, soaked in grease. These were followed by "tallow dips," candles formed from wax rolled around a wick of flax, cotton, or linen thread. The first such candles, used in Elizabethan England, were anything but fragrant; they were made from bullocks' fat, imported from Muscovy. Unlit, they gave off an offensive odor. Lit, they were even more revolting because of the scraps of flesh which remained in the fat. They were eventually improved and purified by melting the tallow in a copper pan and keeping it liquid until the bits of flesh could be skimmed off—and fed to the dogs.

By the early seventeenth century, candles were being scented with roses, juniper, and such spices as cloves. In *The Charitable Physitian,* Philbert Guibert recommended the burning of scented candles as an antidote to infection.

Candlemakers had their own guilds. In Paris, as early as the thirteenth century, a band of traveling candlemakers went from house to house, making candles to order. In England, in the sixteenth century, kitchen fats were saved for the candlemaker. He came at regular intervals to make dark, yellowish candles with rush wicks for the servants—and finer waxen ones with cotton wicks for the gentry in the parlor.

Making your own wax and wick creations can be as simple or as elaborate as you wish. The owner of Candle Mill Village, in East Arlington, Vermont, who has been making candles for over twelve years, has put together a trouble-free kit which provides the novice candlemaker with everything he needs—a six-tube candle mold, wax, colors, scent, wicking, and a specially designed wick holder and pressure pad.

However, you can just as easily shop for blocks of paraffin wax, molds, and other supplies in your local hobby shop. There are even shops like Wick-Work, in Kearny, New Jersey, and Rosalia's Candle Decor, in Parsippany, New Jersey, which are entirely devoted to candlemaking supplies.

You can keep costs down by making your own molds out of tin cans, milk cartons, or the fruit- or fish-shaped metal kitchen molds. Rummaging around at auction sales, garage sales, flea markets, women's exchanges, and so on will turn up a variety of old tin molds, dented but still usable.

For tinting your candles, you can use food dyes, oil colors, powdered coloring material or shavings from colored pure wax crayons. (Small neighbors can be coaxed to give you their broken pieces.) And by adding incense, pine tar, or a few drops of the perfumed oils used in candlemaking, you can get your lighted candles to give off a lovely fragrance.

For step-by-step instructions, equip yourself with a comprehensive, well-illustrated guide to candlemaking. Mary Carey's *Candlemaking* is one such: it contains sections on melting, coloring, scenting and pouring wax; wicks; molds; safety precautions; cleaning up. As a beginner, you will use one of two methods—hand dipping or pouring into molds. The former is the more time-consuming and is limited to tapered candles. Once you have mastered the basic shapes, you can experiment with a variety of types—layered, stacked, sculptured, twisted, and floating.

For Further Reading

Candle Art, by Ray Shaw (William Morrow and Co., Inc., New York, 1973)

The Candle Book, by Carli Laklan (M. Barrows and Co., Inc., New York, 1956)

Creative Candlemaking, by Thelma Newman (Crown Publishers, Inc., New York, 1972)

Candlemaking, by Mary Carey (Golden Press, Western Publishing Co., New York, 1972)

Candle Making, by Maria and Louis di Valentin (Emerson Books, New York, 1974)

EGG DECORATION

No longer merely an Easter pastime for children, egg decoration is now an adult hobby with fascinating possibilities. Some hobbyists show their eggs in museums. Some sell them at high prices. Some look on their finest examples as heirlooms, to be handed down to the next generation. Mrs. Robert Pehlivanian, of Parsippany, New Jersey, feels that egg decoration is a true art form. "Each is a challenge," she told interviewer Joan Burbage, "because I work from the same basic shape and yet they are all individual." One of her fantasies is an excursion balloon, made from a duck egg, with bejeweled drop chains, sapphires, mirrors, and tiny figurines.

Mrs. Rose Pignatura, seventy-six, of Newark, New Jersey, orders her trimmings from many countries. Sometimes she gives her eggs an allover pattern with velvet appliqué. For variety, she cuts a window into an egg and inserts tiny landscapes with flowers or animals.

The most famous of all eggs were created by Karl Fabergé, jeweler to the royal court of Russia. After the murder of Czar Alexander II, nothing could rouse his wife, Maria Alexandrova, from her apathy. Her son, Czar Alexander III, asked Fabergé to create an original egg, as a surprise for his mother on Easter morning. Maria Alexandrova was so charmed with it that, later, Czar Nicholas II commissioned Fabergé to make an egg each Easter for his mother and his wife. After the Revolution, most of the Fabergé eggs found their way into museums and private collections, and many are now in the United States.

It is the ambition of many hobbyists to produce an egg in the manner of Fabergé. Recently, in the Morris Museum of Arts and Sciences, in Morristown, New Jersey, there was a display of twenty-six fabulous eggs, inspired by the master. They were not, however, made from precious metals. Goose, duck, quail, and simple hen eggs were used, decorated with costume jewels and cultured pearls.

If egg decoration appeals to you, you can practice on styrofoam eggs, using trimmings from the hobby shop. Or you can invest in a beginner's kit. But Mrs. Angelo Verdiramo, of Hampton, New Jersey, insists that it is possible to fashion your eggs at little or no cost from materials in your scrapbag. "Almost anything can be used. Ground eggshells mixed with glitter and glue, bits of gift wrap, wallpaper, facial tissues, leather, lace, yarn, fabric, beads or whatever." The tools you will need are also at hand in your home—darning needles, skewers, knitting needles, manicure scissors, pencils, tweezers.

If you enjoy working with others, check whether there is a course in egg decoration at your local arts and crafts center, or in your neighborhood YMCA. Marie and Vera Glowa, of Linden, New Jersey, learned the basics from their mother, and then took advanced courses at a New York YWCA. In love with their hobby, they are now teaching it themselves to students from six to sixty. Several men attend their classes.

If no course is available near you, invest in a copy of *Easter Eggs for Everyone,* by Evelyn Coskey. Everything you need to know about egg decoration, plus some history and lore, is contained in this comprehensive and lavishly illustrated book. Following its instructions, you can begin by using dyes to make striped, plain, checked or plaid eggs, leaf-decorated eggs, scratch-carved eggs, and others. Scratch carving, one of the oldest methods of egg decoration, can be simple or elaborate, depending upon your degree of skill. The design—perhaps a name, an initial, or a simple flower—is first worked out on paper. It is then penciled, very lightly, onto a hard-boiled egg, dyed in a solid color. The motif is scratched onto the egg with a needle or a knife with a fine, sharp point. The result is a white design on a colored egg.

From the simpler eggs, you can proceed to batik process eggs, collage eggs, and novelties. The batik process eggs include *krashanky* and *pysanky,* two of the most beautiful traditional types. *Krashanky,* dyed in brilliant solid colors, may be eaten. *Pysanky* are works of art, handed down from generation to generation. Both kinds originated with the Slavic nations.

Marie Glowa admits that *pysanky* takes patience, but feels that anyone can do it. She draws her designs with a medium hard pencil on eggs that have been warmed to room temperature. She adds successive colors—yellow, orange, and red—with dye dips, starting with the lightest shade.

After each color bath, the egg is dried and beeswax is applied to protect the design. The dyeing proceeds with successively darker colors, ending with black. Finally, the egg is warmed over a candle to melt all the wax, and polished with a tissue to reveal the colors. A coat of shellac is added for protection and gloss.

Collage eggs, says Evelyn Coskey, "can be made even

when you are absolutely certain that there isn't a thing in the house with egg-decorating possibilities." She suggests that you poke around in your kitchen, even in the cleaning closet, and put to use such items as a copper pot-scrubber, used postage stamps, or leftover bits of yarn. "Trim, snip, overlap, or even crochet these things together and glue them onto your egg. Use a colored egg and cover only part of it, or cover it all. You never know what might turn out."

For Further Reading

Fabergé and His Contemporaries, by Henry Hawley (Western Reserve Press, Cleveland, Ohio, 1967)

Painted Easter Eggs, by K.G. Herder (Herder Book Center, New York, 1968)

Easter Eggs for Everyone, by Evelyn Coskey (Abingdon Press, Nashville, Tenn., 1973)

CARVING APPLE-HEAD DOLLS

What cosier place than the kitchen to do a little apple-carving, perhaps with small neighbors agape as they watch. You can make apple-head dolls that are real little personages—Johnny Appleseed, Davy Crockett, or an Indian squaw—or heads that can be used as paperweights.

No special talent is needed for this hobby, although some familiarity with whittling or carving can be helpful. As the materials are cheap, you can afford to practice, discarding your failures and keeping only your best productions.

Although they sell readily at farmers' markets, in novelty shops, and in souvenir stores, apple-head dolls are usually collectors' items because of the time spent in making them. They take about eighteen to twenty hours of work over a period of two to three months to make and dry to perfection. The heads shrink to half their size during the drying process, and the final facial expression is apt to be surprisingly different from what you started with. The mouth and eyes open widely, with comical effect.

Choose your apples carefully, using firm, green fruit with no soft spots. Peel them as smoothly as possible, eliminating all ridges. The actual carving, done with a pocketknife, is simple, about as much as you would do on a pumpkin when making a jack-o'-lantern.

D.C. Cummins, a retired seaman of Sacramento, California, has devised his own tools and methods. He uses a piece of copper, filed into a thin blade, to remove the core. He then stuffs the hole with cotton and glue, so that he can later push out the cheeks or any parts that happen to go in too far.

After shaping the outside of the head with a pocketknife, he hollows it out by working from the neck opening with a pocketknife, a small screwdriver, and a piece of heavy wire with a chisel point filed on it. With a wire hook, he cleans out any loose material. He then cuts in the eyes, mouth, and nostrils. If he makes the teeth from the apple flesh, he uses a thin blade to carve them out. As the head dries, the teeth usually separate, leaving gaps between them.

When the features are complete, the head is immersed in lemon juice for a few hours to prevent discoloration. The apple head is then hung up to dry, or kept in a warm, airy spot from several weeks to a month.

Putting in the finishing touches is the most amusing part of the hobby, for the apple heads seem to come to life under your fingers. Eyes can be made from china-headed pins, round-headed nails, beans, beads, or apple seeds partly painted with white. Porcelain cement also makes good eyes; the pupil can be painted, and the whole eye given a coat of colorless nail varnish to make it shine realistically. The mouth and nostrils can be painted with watercolor paint. Mr. Cummins gets startling effects by making eyes out of the curved surface of a plastic spoon. He makes teeth from bits of plastic fork tines, cemented into place. Wigs for the apple heads can be made from doll hair, real hair, lamb's wool, or knitting yarn.

Mounting the head on a wire body wrapped in old nylon hose allows for a variety of poses. Feet and hands of felt complete the doll. Some hobbyists with knowledge of ceramics sculpt and fire the hands and feet from ceramic clay and attach them firmly to the arm and leg wires.

Some hobbyists become proficient enough to turn out apple-head dolls in fair quantity, for sale. Small dolls, involving a minimum of handwork, bring about $3.50. More elaborate dolls, with ceramic hands and feet, sell from $7.50 up.

The dolls keep surprisingly well. "I have been making them over a period of five years and some of the originals have not changed appreciably during that time," Mildred E. White of Malone, New York, told hobby-writer Bill Newgold. "Recently a man of forty told me he has one in excellent condition made by his mother when he was small; so it is evident that applehead dolls are not a new art."

CHAPTER FIVE

Sitdown Hobbies

CALLIGRAPHY

Easier than drawing or painting, calligraphy or "beautiful writing" is making a comeback, especially among seniors. "No one is too old, or too decrepit, to take up and enjoy this simple hobby, that trains both eye and wrist and can be pursued equally well from one's armchair or bed," says Cecil Chisholm, author of *Retire and Enjoy It.*

You can use calligraphy simply to improve your handwriting and make it beautiful and legible. ("Oh, here's a letter from Aunt Kay—I'd know that exquisite handwriting anywhere!") Or you can letter greeting cards, or wedding and other formal announcements. But whatever your reason for taking it up, you will find the art fascinating and time-consuming. "You're never perfect," says Jeanyee Wong, herself a perfectionist. "You can always do something more and improve." Miss Wong, well known for her designs of UNICEF greeting cards, also uses her calligraphy in book jacket lettering, advertisements, announcements, and invitations.

Louis Strick, director of the Pentalic Corporation which sells italic pens and writing materials, founded the first calligraphy workshop in the United States a few years ago. "Calligraphy is to everyday handwriting as a carefully prepared speech is to casual conversation," he said, offering a three-week course to introduce the art. It was received so enthusiastically that courses began to mushroom around the country. The state of Oregon is the most interested in the teaching of calligraphy, but chances are that you can find a course in your local adult school. The Adult School of Montclair, New Jersey, for instance, offers an excellent course, given by a professional calligrapher; for a fee of $18.00 you can get fundamental knowledge and acquire sufficient technique to make plaques, signs, cards, and formal invitations.

Students of calligraphy are instructed in the italic handwriting which originated in the time of Charlemagne and reached its perfection during the Renaissance in the style known as chancery. This script enables one to form the letters automatically, without pressure of the pen, and therefore saves time. As it is somewhat condensed, it also saves space. Really well written, it is a delight to the eye.

For learning the italic hand, students need an italic nib to get the best results. Many manufacturers have fitted their fountain pens with these nibs. The pen is held at a forty-five degree angle to the writing line. This tilt corresponds to the natural motion of cursive writing and induces legibility.

Because it is traditional, sensible, and pleasing, the italic style is likely to be with us for the foreseeable future. So far, nothing has appeared which will be likely to replace it. Marshall McLuhan, in *The Gutenberg Galaxy,* claims that we are entering a new phase of civilization with accompanying new forms of communication: the Era of the Electronic Man. "There is the strange alphabet used on cheques for the computers at banks and there are highly original graphic art captions of television programs, but these are not relevant to ordinary usage in school and home."

For Further Reading

A Handwriting Manual, by Alfred Fairbank (Transatlantic Arts, Inc., Levittown, N.Y. Third revised edition, 1961)

Italic Calligraphy and Handwriting, Exercises and Text, by Lloyd Reynolds (Pentalic Corp., New York, 1969)

Teach Yourself Handwriting: Chancery Cursive Calligraphy, by John L. Dumpleton (Dover Publications, Inc., New York, 1955)

Note. Pens and all kinds of calligraphic supplies are available from the Pentalic Corporation, 132 W. 22nd St., New York, N.Y. 10011. Catalog on request.

FLY-TYING AND LURE-MAKING

Although there are several hundred firms in this country making lures to catch fish, there is still plenty of scope for the hobbyist. You can take up fly-tying, or making lures, or both. Fly-tying is the making of artificial flies from feathers, tinsel, fabrics, etc. Lures are artificial bait, in such forms as plastic worms.

Big firms put a lot of time and research into their lures. Writer Art Burke tells of a firm that conducted considerable research on squirrel tails before it decided to cover fishing hooks with them. It dressed up two hundred lures with squirrel tails and distributed them among twenty-five testers who were using plain lures. When the results came in, it was obvious that the larger fish had been caught with the squirrel tails.

The hobbyist, however, can substitute experimenting for research and devise lures according to his own fancy. Or he may prefer to take the easy way and follow patterns that have proved successful. He will find hundreds of lures described in fishing books; one such, *Flies,* by J. Edson Leonard, offers bemused hobbyists no less than 2,200 patterns.

In general, fly-tying and lure-making are hobbies for men and boys, but by no means exclusively. Actually, the first artificial lure was made centuries ago by a Benedictine nun. And in Ballyshannon, Ireland, Michael Rogan and his wife, Rita, have trained nine young women in the intricacies of fly-tying—and now conduct a thriving business which is much more than a "cottage industry."

You may think that delicate fingers are a necessity for making such fragile and minuscule things as artificial flies. This is not so. Michael Rogan is described as having "fingers the size of hefty sausages . . . and a massive left thumb." Yet he can produce a tiny and exquisitely fashioned trout fly in less than five minutes.

You need not be a fisherman to make successful flies. Until a few years ago, a community of nuns near Canton, Ohio, supported their convent by making lures—and only one of the nuns had ever fished.

A little rudimentary knowledge of fish will not come amiss, however. For instance, it has long been known that fish feed in any one of three areas of the water—on the surface, from three to six inches below it, and along the bottom. Most lures are designed to travel at one or more of these levels.

A good lure must tempt a fish's appetite, arouse its curiosity—or make it fighting mad. Whether it can distinguish colors is debatable, but most lure-makers believe that color is important. They say that yellow is the most visible color, with red and white next, and fish-scale patterns third.

Fly-tying is not difficult; your first attempt should produce a fly that will take a fish. You can learn the technique from an instruction manual like *The Complete Fly-Tier,* by Reuben B. Cross, or take a few lessons from a professional instructor. George Bodmer, owner of Bodmer's Fly Shop in Colorado Springs, Colorado, teaches courses for both beginners and advanced tiers.

The beginner's course usually consists of five classes and covers the fundamentals. The advanced course consists of individual instruction. "Tying flies requires about 25 per cent knowledge and 75 per cent practice," says George. How long it takes to learn varies with the individual.

The tools for this hobby are comparatively inexpensive, but it will pay you to buy the best quality you can afford. As a beginner you will need a vise of the special kind made for fly-tying; hackle pliers for removing from a rooster's neck the tufts of feathers used as the legs of the fly (the necks, skinned and dried, are available at fishing-tackle stores); scissors, preferably two pairs, one for heavy work and one for delicate; a spool for holding thread; a bodkin or dubbing needle. If you buy these items separately, your tools will cost you from $25.00 up. You can save by buying a beginner's kit for from $12.00 up, depending upon the quality of the tools.

The materials needed for fly-tying and lure-making are feathers, thread, tinsel, floss, fabrics, raffia, cork, horsehair, etc., depending upon what kind of fly you want to make. At times you will need ingenuity to come up with a specific color or texture. Michael Rogan was once asked by an American to copy a fly whose body was a peculiar shade of grayish brown. Nothing he had in stock was anything like the color needed. He eventually solved his problem by using some fur shed by a grayish-brown kitten.

If you hope to make a profit with your hobby, it will

pay you to invest in one or two instruction books; the greater variety of flies you learn to make, the better your chance of filling lucrative special orders. The books will teach you "tricks of the trade" which will help you to make flies of superior quality. You will also find it advisable to browse around frequently in fishing supply stores and ask "What's new?" In recent years, many modern materials have come into use—brilliant fluorescent plastics, for instance, are cheaper than tinsel and do not tarnish. There are also new detergents which do an excellent job of degreasing feathers; this is necessary if you want to dye them.

To ensure making salable flies, find out what kinds of fishing are available in your neighborhood. Get to know the fishing enthusiasts and find out what type of fly they use.

Where can you sell what you produce? "Anyone who can tie a good fly can find a market for it," says George Bodmer. The beginner usually does best by selling to local sporting goods stores and fly shops. Later, when he can produce large quantities, he can contact jobbers through owners of local sporting goods shops. If he prefers to sell privately, the hobbyist can advertise in sports and outdoors magazines, such as *Field and Stream, Camping Journal,* and *Fishing World.*

Dorothy Nix, of Colorado Springs, Colorado, is one of a number of housewives who find fly-tying a satisfactory outlet for creative talents as well as a source of extra income. "A person who is really good can earn as much, or more, in 25 to 30 hours than she can at most jobs working 40 hours," she says.

For Further Reading

Fly-Tying, by William Bayard Sturgis (Charles Scribner's Sons, New York, 1940)

Art Flick's Master Fly-Tying Guide, by Art Flick (Crown Publishers, Inc., New York, 1972)

Bodmer's Fly Shop Catalog No. 2 (Free. 2404 East Boulder, Colorado Springs, Colo. 80901)

Fly-Tying–Materials–Tools–Techniques, by Helen Shaw (The Ronald Press Co., New York, 1963)

WHITTLING AND WOODCARVING

Sit-down hobbies par excellence, whittling and woodcarving know no season and no age limit. Charles Wright of California, a retiree, began with some cautious whittling but was soon so fascinated that he became "a carving addict." One of his recent showpieces is an American Indian and buffalo scene, carved from black walnut worth $800.

John F. Thomas, a Long Island City businessman, says that "executives can whittle their worries away," and even keeps a set of carving tools and a few wooden blocks in his office. His whittling creations range from model ships to birds. On weekends, as many as a dozen pre-teen-agers, all potential woodcarvers, join him in his basement workshop.

Women are every bit as good at whittling as men. Millie Miller, of West Branch, Michigan, has won herself the nickname "Millie the Chiseler." She has been carving for over twenty-five years, ever since her son brought her a fireplace log that suggested possibilities. Chipping away at it with her paring knife, Millie produced a frog on a log. Today, working with more sophisticated tools and in a variety of woods, she carves whatever she pleases. Her specialty is totem poles; Millie may be the only female totem pole carver in the land.

If you are attracted to the warmth and beauty of wood, the simplest way to use it in a hobby is by whittling. You will need only a sharp penknife or jackknife and a piece of wood about the size of a cotton spool. Sharpen the knife by pressing it, with a circular motion, onto wet or oiled stone. If it has previously been nicked or spoiled, begin by sharpening it with a fine file or emery paper on a board.

Soft and semi-hard woods are easier to shave than others. Your local lumberyard will have cut-offs (remnants), economically priced. White pine is easiest to handle, but lime, holly, and plum are all excellent for whittling.

Practice until you can control the knife properly, keeping your fingers safely behind the cutting edge and always protecting your thumb. Sometimes you will have to shave off a sizable bit of wood before you see the desired shape emerging. Because of the shavings, which tend to fly around, it is a good idea to whittle on a porch or in a suitable outdoor spot, preferably in old clothes. If you must remain indoors, station your chair in the center of a good-sized dropcloth for easy cleanup.

Whittling can bring you happy associations. After a decline of a few decades, this old craft is flourishing again. Whittlers and woodcarvers have their own organization, the National Woodcarvers Association, in Cincinnati, Ohio. They have their own bi-monthly magazine, *Chit and Chat,* which is also read in England, Scotland, Denmark, South Africa, and Australia. In 1973, they opened their own museum, the National Carvers Museum, in Monument, Colorado. Currently it displays over two thousand carvings from all over the United States, which range from religious figures to fine inlays and come in every kind of wood from pine to maple.

Speaking of the fascination of wood, Ed Gallenstein, president of the National Woodcarvers Association, says; "There's something about wood, a kind of warm attraction. It's alive, you know. It expands and contracts with moisture, and sometimes a crack will appear, and you'll wonder what to do. Then the next day it'll be gone." Once wood has you in its thrall, you will inevitably progress from whittling to woodcarving.

You should begin by making a preliminary study of woods, with particular reference to their graining, texture, hardness, and such other qualities as will influence your carving. Balsa, for instance, is a poor choice; it is too soft and does not last. Cherry, a hard wood, will give excellent results—but not until the carver is familiar with the use of gouges, chisels, and mallets. Oak, although the most durable wood, is best avoided; it is very difficult for a beginner to handle.

Until recently, instruction in woodcarving was hard

to come by. Today, however, you may find courses given in arts and crafts centers, adult schools, and the like. The Caldwell Center of Community and Continuing Education, in Caldwell, New Jersey, for instance, offers an evening course, Sculpture in Wood, for a fee of $25.00.

If you do not find a course in your vicinity, you can turn to books. There are many excellent ones which will help you learn the techniques of woodcarving. And if you know of any experienced woodcarver in your neighborhood, you might approach him for tips or advice.

Provided the budget will run to it (wood is currently expensive), you can get all the wood you need at lumberyards, some of which offer blocks suitable for carving. It is practical, too, to browse around in junk and secondhand stores for discarded furniture. This will often yield choice pieces of cherry, maple, or teakwood.

Tools need not be an expensive item. Although there is a great variety of carving tools on the market, most are only needed for the very fine or intricate work. The beginner will get along nicely with either a beginner's kit (priced from $10.00 up) or with his own assemblage of carving chisels, raps, mallets, and sharpening stones. If they are to do their job, carving tools must be kept sharp, and new tools must be sharpened before they can be used.

You will need a workbench or sturdy table, with a strong vise attached to it. Some pieces of carving need to be held in place by a bench or lag screw from underneath the surface of the bench.

What you carve will depend upon whether you are making something for a gift, to sell, or for your own pleasure and keeping. If your carving is to be a gift, consult the giftee; he may prefer a decoy duck to even the most comical of carved cats. If you expect to sell your carvings, visit fairs and gift shops to find out which carved wooden items are most in demand.

Relief carvings, a simple type of woodcarving, make highly acceptable gifts or sale items. To carve in relief, a design is traced on paper and transferred to the wood. The surplus wood is then cut away to a depth of an eighth of an inch, so that the design stands out clearly. If the carving is made on a thin piece of wood, it can be fashioned into a plaque. Trays, box lids, bookends, bowls and pieces of furniture can be carved in relief very effectively.

For Further Reading

Wood Carving and Whittling Made Easy, by Franklin H. Gottshall (The Macmillan Co., New York, 1963)

Ben Hunt's Big Book of Whittling (The Macmillan Co., New York, 1970)

Woodcarving, by Allan Durst (Studio Publications, Viking Press, New York, 1948)

Book of Woodcarving, by John Lacy (Prentice-Hall, Inc., New York, 1953)

How To Do Wood Carving, by John Lacy (Arco Publishing Co., New York, 1954)

JIGSAW PUZZLING

An engrossing hobby to share or to enjoy alone is solving jigsaw puzzles. If you haven't done one since you were a kid, today's sophisticated beauties will surprise you. The subjects are unusual, artistic, informative, inspirational.

Put together Tadasky's "Whirling Discs" or Gauguin's "Tahitian Landscape"—and you'll be hooked. You'll be in good company. Celebrities like the Duchess of Windsor and the Rockefellers dote on jigsaw puzzles.

The most popular size contains 750 pieces, ideal for laying out on a bridge table. Other puzzles have as many as 2,000 pieces. If money is no object, you can have one made to order to cover your billiard table.

Jigsaw puzzles have a long history, full of ups and downs. The ancient Egyptians assembled giant puzzles in the form of mosaics. Jigsaws fascinated the Orient centuries ago. Women and girls were not permitted to try them. They could only stand at a respectful distance and watch as men and boys worked huge puzzles on the floors.

The first European jigsaw puzzle was cut by hand in the 1760's. Puzzles became educational and were soon very popular in the classroom. "Dissected maps" were favorites. The sea, or the neighboring countries, formed the frame of the puzzle map and were left in one piece. But puzzles were very expensive, so John Spillsbury, the first puzzle maker, offered dissected maps "without the sea" at bargain prices. This was to save wood; in those days, mahogany and poplar were much used.

By the 1850's, the puzzles got the name "jigsaw" from the tool used to carve them. It was a vertically reciprocating saw, used to cut irregular patterns. At this time, too, soft wood began to be used, and jigsaw puzzles became cheaper.

About 1910 there was a craze for puzzles among adults, and their popularity continued up to World War I. The subjects were landscapes, seascapes, sporting scenes, scenes from Charles Dickens' novels, topical events, and royalty.

By 1920, jigsaw puzzles had become popular in the United States. During the Great Depression, thousands of jobless men and women turned to them for cheap entertainment. But puzzles began to be neglected with the advent of radio and, later, television.

Today jigsaw puzzles are again enjoying popularity. Some years ago, a graphic expert, Robert Lewin, brought a circular puzzle home from England. Friends of the family found it so absorbing that Robert and his wife, Katie, seldom had a chance to work on it themselves.

The idea of creating adult puzzles sprang up almost at once in Katie's fertile mind. Before long she was in business, selling novel and very beautiful puzzles. Because of her lifetime interest in wildlife and conservation, she named her puzzles Springbok, after the African antelope.

Subjects for the new puzzles were not easy to come by. "I've walked through thousands of miles of American and European museums, looking for the painting with just the right ingredients—one that would make a puzzle beautiful and difficult enough to satisfy an adult appetite," Katie says. The resulting puzzles offer an impressive choice. They cover fine art, modern art, moon myths, wild life, decorative art, and maps of special interest. Salvador Dali has created at least one subject for Springbok, and the nation's greatest wildlife experts have suggested such subjects as tropical birds, butterflies, the mushroom puzzle, and "Last Chance on Earth; America's Endangered Wild Life."

Note. When you have exhausted Springbok and Eaton puzzles, two of the best and most popular types on the market, you may like to investigate wooden jigsaw puzzles, hand cut, one piece at a time. A large and unusual variety is obtainable from the Glencraft Shop, 1059 N. River Road, South Windham, Maine 04082. The shop will send you on request a brochure about these puzzles which are collectors' items of the future.

SCRIMSHAW

For a really unique hobby, try scrimshaw. This unusual handcraft of yesteryear, in which designs were carved on whale teeth and elephant tusks, is making a comeback today. Charming scrimshaw articles, including earrings, pendants, tie tacks, and rings, are to be found in gift shops, especially in the New England states.

No one is certain where the word "scrimshaw" originated, but it may have come from the Dutch *scrimsharder,* a lazy fellow. In whaling-ship days, when a whaleman wasn't actively chasing a whale, he had time on his hands and might conceivably have thought himself a lazy fellow.

Laziness ended when the whaleman learned the art of scrimshaw from the Eskimos, and, in turn, passed it on to other sailors. The Eskimos of Alaska were expert carvers. "Once," says Seon Manley, in *Adventures in Making: Romance of Crafts Around the World,* "an explorer asked an Eskimo to draw him a picture of a walrus hunt. The Eskimo threw down the pencil angrily; it was much too difficult for him. Instead, he took up a piece of walrus bone, and in a few minutes he had engraved all the details of the exciting scene."

Sailors in the nineteenth century learned to make pipes, earrings, buckles, needlecases—even stays for ladies' corsets! Besides such useful items, they carved miniatures of seals, dogs, polar bears—and their favorite kind of whale.

Even if you are "all thumbs," you can master the art of scrimshaw—with patience. First try your hand on a piece of soapstone, and discover what happens when you "get the feel" of your material. In former times, you would have progressed to carving on whale teeth and elephant tusks. But today, because of the ban on whale hunting (observed by all countries except Russia and Japan) and also on elephant hunting, such materials are hard to find. Contemporary scrimshaw artists are using shells and other hard, natural substances. (The more persistent hobbyists search for ivory in the form of old piano keys, or the shoehorns, hairbrushes, and other articles in which ivory was used by previous generations.)

The safest and most practical tool for you to employ is the scorper used by professional ivory carvers. This is a chisel with a fine, tapering, triangular point and a mushroom handle. It needs to be sharpened often while you work.

You might also use an "eskimo style," which you can make yourself without much difficulty. You can work at any sturdy table, using a clamp-on vise. You will need a wood dowel ⅜″ by ½″ by 3″. Round one end of the dowel and cut a notch about ¾″ from the end. This notch will help your finger keep a firm grip on the style. Drill a hole through the rounded end of the dowel, using a hand or electric drill and bit. Then saw a nail in half with a hacksaw and sharpen both ends with a file. Cement the nail into the hole. By using the eskimo style as a pencil you can engrave all kinds of complicated designs.

Traditionally, whales' teeth were carved with marine subjects, although nineteenth century sailors also liked to carve flags, birds, and castles. You may choose any subject, provided it is not too elaborately detailed.

The final process in scrimshaw is inking the lines.

Take a pen with a fine, elongated point and draw along the *inside* of the lines with India ink. If you wish, you can use poster paint in other colors. Finish by rubbing the object with a piece of fine sandpaper to remove any ink which may have run outside the lines.

For Further Reading

All Hands Aboard Scrimshawing, by Marius Barbeau (Peabody Museum, Salem, Mass., 1973)

Scrimshaw and Scrimshanders: Whales and Whalemen, by E.N. Flayderman (N. Flayderman and Co., Inc., New Milford, Conn., 1972)

Scrimshaw, by Carson I. Ritchie (Sterling Publishing Co., New York, 1972)

The Scrimshaw Book, by Charles R. Meyer (Henry Z. Walck, Inc., New York, 1975)

CHAPTER SIX

Hobbies to Entertain With

CLOWNING

If you have ever had a secret yearning to be "on stage," now is your chance. As a clown, a mime, a ventriloquist, a puppeteer, you can escape into a world of fantasy and give untold pleasure to children and grown-ups in homes, hospitals, and elsewhere.

Clowns in great variety have entertained us since the *dangas,* dwarf clowns, amused the rulers of Egypt thousands of years ago. As fools, court jesters, gleemen, mummers, and fairground mountebanks, they have wandered all over the world through the ages. Today they are found largely in circuses, working in the audience or getting themselves mixed up in the other acts. Some have elaborate and even dangerous routines; they perform on a wire or a trapeze, on weird bicycles, and even on stilts.

But clowning as a hobby is a simpler matter, needing little but a comical costume, exaggerated makeup, and a repertoire of antics, jokes, and absurdities. If you wish, you can remain anonymous, known only by a nickname. If you are bashful, you can, like Emmett Kelly, better known as Willy the Clown, do your act without once opening your mouth. Willy, says John Hornby in *Clowns Through the Ages,* "is a sad and lonely wanderer who drifts around the arena, lighting little campfires and salvaging tiny bits of rubbish with the greatest of care. . . . His clothes are a rag-bag collection, falling to pieces but held together by pins and pieces of string."

Begin by devising your costume and makeup. You may like to clown in whiteface, with a funny, painted mouth and a red nose, small as a cherry. You may imitate the French *Augustes,* wearing a patched and baggy suit and enormous, bumpy boots. You can get ideas by browsing around in a theatrical and masquerade costumer's store, where there are thousands of costumes to look over. You can leaf through "fancy dress" pattern books. And you can dream up some eye-catching accessories—perhaps a huge umbrella, a battered gilt hand mirror, a fantastic rainhat.

Before you give your show, try to find out a little about your audience. Learn some of their names, and their interests and weaknesses. Then think up a few "insults" to toss at them. Teasing—of a broad, good-humored kind—is part of the stock-in-trade of the clown. In ancient Greece, clowns called *parasites* were invited to do their acts in return for their supper. They teased their hosts and the guests, even the most important.

You can address members of your audience by their names, and poke gentle fun. "(Hi, Billy, I have a message from your dog. He wants to know where you hid his bone." "Joanie, you'd make a fine clown—all those missing teeth!" "Did you knit that new bedjacket yourself, Mrs. Jones? Are those dropped stitches, or part of the pattern?")

Work up your act, including jokes, riddles, bits of neighborhood news, and add, subtract, and revise occasionally to keep it fresh. You can sometimes produce a surprise from your capacious pocket, tossing packages of candy or small felt animals into the audience. You can invite them to "sing along" with you, making your own voice off-key to provoke groans and laughter.

If you feel a need for formal instruction in clowning, you may find a course which will help you achieve professional finish. In New York City, for instance, the New Center for Theater Arts, in the 92nd Street YM-YWHA, offers a semester in clowning for $70.00. It includes solo and ensemble clowning; slapstick and comedy falls; makeup; costuming; pantomime, etc. "See and know yourself better as you learn the special craft of laughter," the catalog entices. This particular course is aimed at young people, but your local adult school might arrange to give such a course, on request.

FOR FURTHER READING

The Clown, by Emmett Kelly (Prentice-Hall, Inc., New York, 1954)

Clowns Through the Ages, by John Hornby (Henry Z. Walck, Inc., New York, 1965)

MAGIC

Providing you have patience and are ready for hours of practice, you can make conjuring, popularly known as "magic," a fascinating and profitable hobby. You will be in demand at children's parties and fund-raising events, and in homes and hospitals for children and adults.

Magic, which derives its name from the Magi, is one of the oldest forms of entertainment. It is also the one theater art which is completely international. The old and basic feats are performed by the magicians of all nations. An interest in them persists; many of the tricks used in ancient Greece and Rome are performed today in almost the same way.

The successful conjurer needs no special talents but must have a pleasing personality, and the assurance that comes from knowing that he has mastered his tricks in every detail. He need not originate his own tricks, for there are thousands of magic feats already invented from which he can put together his program. But he should have sufficient originality to make new combinations from old ideas.

He must also be able to build up a smooth line of "patter" to accompany his tricks. This patter is a necessary part of his act; while he directs attention elsewhere, his hands are performing the trick. "It is the same technique employed by the child at home who says excitedly, 'Look over there, Mother! What is that on the tree?' While she looks in the direction he is pointing, he steals the cherry off the cake she has just been icing." So says hobby writer Margaret Mulac.

Costly apparatus is not necessary; there are hundreds of tricks which can be performed with inexpensive equipment. It is a good plan, however, to send for the latest catalogs of one or more firms that make or distribute magic goods. The catalogs will be helpful when you need to order any standard equipment for your act.

The first essential for the beginning conjurer is a good textbook, one which covers dress, showmanship, technique, equipment, as well as giving detailed instructions for performing a variety of tricks. See what your local library has to offer, and invest in the book which most appeals to you. You will need to keep it at hand for reference. A good choice for the novice conjurer is *The Amateur Magician's Handbook* by Henry Hay.

You will find it easiest to begin with card tricks, which need little equipment other than marked cards or special packs. Assiduous practice in manipulating the cards will give you the deftness needed for all types of sleight-of-hand magic.

There are even card tricks which do not require sleight-of-hand. During World War II, when the playing card industry offered its services to the Recreation Department of the Red Cross, it was told that many hospitalized soldiers would like to learn card tricks which they could perform from bed or a wheelchair. The inventors came up with a collection of tricks based on simple optical illusions and elementary arithmetic.

When he has learned to handle cards expertly, the hobbyist can progress to the more complicated pocket and apparatus tricks. The Abracadabra Magic Shop, in Colonia, New Jersey, known as "the magicians' second home," puts out a "super giant magic catalog," listing dozens of tricks which hobbyists can learn to perform.

Another branch of magic within the scope of the beginner is chemical magic, tricks which are really dressed-up chemical experiments, involving such things as hot air, sound vibrations, magnetism, etc. You do not need to have special knowledge of chemistry; all you require are the necessary formulas, a collection of relatively cheap chemicals and the simplest of apparatus. Provided you follow the instructions carefully, the chemicals themselves will give the performance for you. You will have to supply the patter; in it, you can explain the chemical effects but *not* the chemical reactions.

When you reach the point of giving magic performances in public, arrange to "travel light." Choose tricks which you can do with everyday household items and no special apparatus. Work from a suitcase if you can. If not, provide yourself with a table sufficiently large to hold your needs comfortably. A card table is usually sufficient. Later, you may want to invest in a professional "magician's table," complete with black velvet top, gold fringe, and a secret well for making handkerchiefs, cards, etc., disappear and appear.

How much working space you need will depend upon your act, your audience, and the place where you are giving the entertainment. Most magicians like to have plenty of space around them, so that no one will be able to peep over their shoulders or stand behind their backs. If possible, get an advance look at the room in which you will work; it may be possible to rearrange it to your satisfaction.

A word of caution. Never let yourself be persuaded to explain your tricks. Remember that they are your stock-in-trade. Whether they are amateur or professional, magicians keep the secrets of their tricks confined to their own special circle. They form clubs, exchange ideas, try out their acts on one another, and are often generous enough to help inexperienced magicians improve their performances. If there is a Magicians' Society in your area, write to the secretary and ask what qualifications are needed to be accepted for membership.

For Further Reading

Card Tricks for Beginners, by Harry Baron (Emerson Books, Inc., New York, 1970)

Card Tricks for Everyone, by Ellis Stanyor (Emerson Books, Inc., New York, 1968)

Magic Digest, by George B. Anderson (Follett Educational Corporation, Chicago, 1972)

Teach Yourself Magic, by J. Elsden Tuffs (Emerson Books, Inc., New York, 1970)

The Amateur Magician's Handbook, by Henry Hay (Crowell, New York, 1972)

Dunninger's Complete Encyclopedia of Magic, by Joseph Dunninger (Lyle Stuart, New York, 1967)

Magic in Mind: Mental Magic Tricks, by Bill Severn (Henry Z. Walck, Inc., New York, 1974)

Magic with Cards, by Frank Garcia and George Schindler (Henry Z. Walck, Inc., New York, 1975)

VENTRILOQUISM

As entertainment at parties, and in hospitals and homes, nothing beats ventriloquism. Become a ventriloquist and you will be sure of a welcome. And because of popular misconceptions about the art, you will have few competitors.

Ventriloquism is the art of using the voice in such a way that the sounds seem to be produced at a distance from the speaker. The origin of the word, which comes from *venter,* belly, and *loquus,* speaker, suggests that the voice comes from the speaker's stomach, but this is not so. His words are produced in the usual way, but his breath is allowed to escape slowly, the tones being muffled by the narrowing of the glottis, the opening between the vocal cords in the larynx.

The art of ventriloquism is an ancient one, traces of which are found in Egyptian and Greek archaeology. Eurycles of Athens was the most celebrated Greek ventriloquist. His imitators were sometimes called after him, *eurycleides;* more often they were called *engastrimanteis,* or belly prophets.

It is probable that the priests of ancient times practiced ventriloquism expertly. This would explain such apparent miracles as the speaking statues of the Egyptians, the Greek oracles, and the stone in the river Pactolus, the sound of which put robbers to flight. Although no one can account for it, many of today's underdeveloped races—the Maoris, Eskimos, Zulus, and others—are skilled ventriloquists. Birds like the chickadee and dove are also natural ventriloquists.

If you are prepared to practice day in, day out, you can become quite a passable ventriloquist in a gratifyingly short time. Practice in front of a mirror, sitting firmly, holding your jaw rigid, and keeping your lips slightly apart with your teeth almost touching. You will find that you can move your tongue freely inside your mouth but will at first have difficulty in producing any sound. Do not worry about letters or words at first, but concentrate on making a grunting noise from your chest.

Peter Brough, a well-known ventriloquist, advises his students to start with the alphabet, paying particular attention to those letters which are the most difficult to pronounce—B, P, V, and W. As soon as you can say short, very simple sentences, practice a sentence like "Bring back black and brown boots, bread and butter, and a bottle of beer from Birmingham." Keep repeating it until you are confident that you have mastered the letter B. Then invent your own nonsense sentences, emphasizing the other difficult letters in turn.

When you reach the stage where you can hold a long conversation with yourself, asking and answering questions briskly and clearly, you will be ready to practice altering the pitch of your voice, trying to make it both very high and very low. This is an important part of the ventriloquist's art, for by altering the pitch he can get the effects he wants.

As soon as you are satisfied that you can "throw" your voice distinctly and alter the pitch as you wish, you can try working with a prop. You might begin by contriving a "dummy" out of your right hand, painting on eyes and manipulating the fingers so that they look like a mouth. You can, however, make your act effective without using a prop if you make your voice appear to come from some amusing and unexpected place—a coffeepot, a plant, a baby, a telephone, or the family cat.

As soon as you are ready for it, a ventriloquist's dummy will improve your act amazingly. Sometimes difficult to find, they may be obtained from Juro Celebrity Dolls, 12 East 18th St., New York, N.Y. 10010, which stocks the most popular dummies—Danny O'Day, Hayley O'Hara, Charlie McCarthy, Mortimer

Snerd, and others. You can also purchase a ventriloquist package which includes a 24″ Danny O'Day; an extra baseball outfit; and an "instant ventriloquism" instruction recording.

You will need to create a voice for your dummy, making it different from your own and as distinctive as possible. You will need, too, to develop a personality for him. Imitate the professional ventriloquist and think of your dummy as your *partner;* if you think and act as if he were a real person, you will easily persuade the audience that he is alive.

Finally, work from a script, giving the best lines to your dummy so as to focus attention on him and away from yourself. Learn the script by heart, because not having to pause for words will give you confidence. Unless you have a special gift for speaking extempore, you might "dry up" and ruin your act.

For Further Reading

Ventriloquism for Beginners, by Douglas Houlden (A.S. Barnes and Co., Inc., Cranbury, N.J., 1967)

Ventriloquism Made Easy, by J. Mendoza (Wehman Brothers, Hackensack, N.J., 1955)

ORIGAMI

A hobby which you can use for your own pleasure, or to delight audiences, origami is the art of folding objects—fish, animals, flowers, birds—from a single sheet of paper, without cutting or pasting. The name is derived from two Japanese words; *ori,* fold, and *kami,* paper. Origami is far removed from kindergarten paper play; it is a sophisticated art. The Spanish philosopher Miguel de Unamuno enchanted small watchers with his originality and was perhaps the best-known European origamist. Leonardo da Vinci folded a replica of the typical paper airplane of today. And Lewis Carroll, author of *Alice in Wonderland,* amused the royal children of the Duchess of Albany by folding paper fishing boats for them and teaching them to make paper pistols.

In Japan, a country which has a deep respect for paper and produces handmade paper of rare quality, origami is used to fashion delicate ornaments to tie onto gifts for special occasions. It is also used in celebrations. On Boys' Day, paper carp are raised in the air and carried around.

Origami master Akira Yoshizawa is responsible for the current worldwide interest in this art. From boyhood, he was always excited about origami. At the end of World War II, he had an irresistible offer; the editor of an illustrated weekly wanted an origamist to produce the twelve signs of the zodiac. The figures made by Akira were so lifelike and exquisite that they caused a sensation. Today Akira is world-famous; his art has inspired thousands of artists and hobbyists, and books on his technique are available in public libraries.

As a hobby, origami is spellbinding and inexpensive.

It requires patience, perseverance—and paper. You can buy special origami paper, imported from Japan. Available usually in seven-inch squares, it is perfect for folding into small models. (Sources of this paper are listed in *The Art of Origami,* by Samuel Randlett.)

Other usable papers are gift-wrap, shelf paper, brown and colored wrapping paper, bond typing paper in pastel shades, airmail paper, aluminum foil, and aluminum foil backed with kraft paper. Whatever the type, the paper must be thin and must take a sharp crease.

A piece of Masonite about a foot square makes a convenient working surface. Paper can be squared with scissors or a knife, but it is worth investing in a 12″ paper-cutter, which does the job simply. These are available in office equipment and photographic supply stores.

You will also need small, sharp, straight scissors for detail work, and a razor or Exacto knife will sometimes be useful. Although origami experts insist that no cuts must be made and no paste must be used, exceptions are sometimes made if the effect produced is spectacular enough to justify the liberty taken.

Round eyes can be made with a quarter-inch dime store paper punch. Or a one-eighth of an inch ticket punch can be obtained from the McGill Metal Products Company, 11 West 42nd St., New York, N.Y. 10036.

Origami books give step-by-step instructions; careful preliminary study of the fold-chart for the object you wish to make is necessary. Symbols are frequently used in the instructions, and Akira Yoshizawa's code of lines and arrows is rapidly becoming the international language of origami. In Samuel Randlett's *The Art of Origami,* Akira's code is used throughout.

The beginner should start with something simple, like folding paper into a box. He can progress to the study of more advanced origami folds and eventually produce more sophisticated objects. When he has developed enough skill to master the traditional Japanese sitting crane, he will be well on his way to having mastered the first stages of origami. Henceforth he will be limited only by his own ingenuity. Today's experts are extraordinarily successful with miniature animals, birds, insects, and all kinds of inanimate objects.

The demonstration of origami is fine entertainment for parties, and excellent therapy for the sick. While Akira Yoshizawa was on a goodwill tour of New Zealand and visited mental institutions, the patients were entranced by the magical way in which he transformed squares of paper into butterflies and birds. Akira himself would like to see the peoples of the world busy with origami. "For when we are using our hands effectively," he says, "our hearts are most at peace."

For Further Reading

The Art of Origami, by Samuel Randlett (E.P. Dutton and Co., Inc., New York, 1961)

The Art of Chinese Paper Folding: For Young and Old, by

Maying Soong (Harcourt, Brace and Co., New York, 1948)

How to Make Origami, edited by Isao Honda (McDowell, Obolensky, New York, 1959)

The Paper Book, by Don Munson and Allianora Rosse (Charles Scribner's Sons, New York, 1972)

Creating with Paper, by Pauline Johnson (University of Washington Press, Seattle, Wash., 1966)

New Adventures in Origami, by Robert Harbin (Funk and Wagnalls Publishing Co., New York, 1972)

CHAPTER SEVEN

Hobbies from Nature

DISH GARDENING

If you haven't the patience to follow the fashion and create gardens in small-necked bottles, glass jars, and brandy snifters, you can still make effective miniatures. Use the more manageable open dishes filched from your kitchen or china closet—salad bowls, ceramic jelly molds, plain and fancy casseroles, even "antique" moustache cups. A shallow baking dish, planted with periwinkle, makes a delightful centerpiece, and an oversize coffee cup is a charming home for peperomia and sansevieria.

While the Japanese are the most skilled in making miniature gardens, the British are a good second. When Queen Elizabeth II saw her first miniature garden, she was so captivated that she ordered some to be made for the state banquets that followed her coronation. On the guest tables, conventional flowers were used, but at the Queen's table, in a place of honor, was an enchanting little woodland scene, housed in a porcelain bowl.

Dish gardening, while a challenge, involves little hard work. The only "digging" necessary can be done with a table fork. Any good potting soil can be used, but be careful about watering. A dish garden, planted as it is in an open container, must be watered fairly often to keep it moist.

Dish gardens are flexible enough to suit moods and seasons. If you tire of your garden, you can gently lift out some of the plants and replace them with something new. You can have a short-term garden by sliding a pack of bedding plants—dwarf marigolds are beautiful—into a shallow casserole. Set in the sun, the flowers will bloom well, and when they grow too big for the container you can replant them outdoors.

You can have a conventional garden with indoor or tropical plants like philodendron, dracaena, gloxinia, etc. For height and background the small sansevieria makes a pleasing contrast to leafy plants. Do not obscure the individual plants by overcrowding, and take the growth factor into consideration, keeping the taller plants at the back of the dish.

Your garden will be a conversation piece if you give it a theme. Make it a rock garden, with a sandy path leading to a tiny cottage. Build up a number of flattish stones on various levels, and cover the soil with a layer of granite chippings. Miniature pines and firs look well in this kind of garden.

A cactus garden is eye-catching and requires a minimum of watering. As cacti grow in arid climates, make your garden resemble a desert scene. If you are skilled in ceramics, add a tiny figure of a Mexican peon, leading his burro.

For a miniature woodland glade, you will need a group of little trees, underplanted with violets and primroses. Seedlings of many kinds of trees can be used successfully but, eventually, when they have grown too tall, they will have to be replaced.

Tempting though they are, avoid overloading your garden with ornaments and figures; the tiny plants will need space to grow in and as much soil as possible. Do not add anything that is not strictly miniature. One hobbyist tried putting a little fish in a pool as a realistic touch. But the fish looked terribly out of proportion and did not survive long in the shallow water.

Plan your garden carefully before you start, making sure that you will be able to get the plants and ornaments you visualize. You will find that almost everything you need can be bought in a good florist's—even miniature trees and rose bushes. There are also various shrubs and plants that will compose a pretty landscape.

In toy stores, junk shops, and china stores, you may find china or pottery ornaments that will give you different kinds of dish gardens. You might, for instance, come upon a Japanese pagoda, a Swiss chalet, or an English cottage. You can add realism by making items which you cannot find in stores. Fire cement, which is easy to mold, makes excellent walls, bridges, sundials, and crazy pavement. Bake the object stone-hard and then paint it with oil or poster paint.

Dish gardens cannot be expected to last for more than two seasons before their plants get too big. You may be able to make them last longer by thinning out the larger plants. Stand your indoor gardens near a window where they will benefit from the light, and turn them regularly so that the plants will not grow lopsided from bending toward the sun. And besides regular watering, once a week use a fine sprayer on the foliage of your gardens.

For Further Reading

Miniature Plants, Indoors and Out, by Jack Kramer (Charles Scribner's Sons, New York, 1971)

Miniature Flower Arrangements and Planting, by Lois Wilson (Hawthorn Books, Inc., New York, 1970)

Fun with Terrarium Gardening, by Virginia and George A. Elbert (Crown Publishers, Inc., New York, 1973)

GROWING BONSAI

A challenging art, bonsai growing takes a gentle touch, time, and infinite patience. But when, after a few seasons, you have completed your project, you have something special—the very essence of a tree, imprisoned in a small pot, to be enjoyed indoors.

Originating in China over a thousand years ago,

bonsai was developed in Japan. During the thirteenth century, the Japanese simply collected and potted trees that had been dwarfed by nature. But when demand for the tiny trees began to exceed the supply, Japanese gardeners started to train bonsai from native trees. Over the years, they developed standards of shape and form which have become classic.

Choosing the plants to be trained as bonsai is an art in Japan. Collectors go out into fields and woodlands, searching for windblown specimens which can be successfully transplanted. They come across some of their best finds while scrambling up seaside cliffs, hills, and mountains.

Americans, with a much freer style, have taken Oriental styles and applied them to plants never grown in Japan. Not all plants are equally effective as bonsai. The avocado, with its overly large leaves, will look out of proportion; sycamores also develop leaves which are too large.

To produce a realistic illusion of a mature tree, look for the following characteristics:

Small leaves or needles
Short internodes or distances between leaves
Attractive bark or roots
Branching characteristics for good twig forms.

The easiest way for the beginner to obtain bonsai is to buy nursery stock and develop his own. Those plants that are native to the area where he lives often make fine subjects for bonsai.

Three basic operations are necessary in bonsai culture to establish the basic form—pruning, nipping, and wiring. Detailed instructions for these operations are given in the *Home and Gardening Bulletin No. 206,* put out by the United States Department of Agriculture.

The basic tools needed include a pair of sharp hook-and-blade pruning shears; a garden trowel; blunt sticks; a pair of sturdy wire-cutters; copper wire of various lengths; a sprinkling can. Also useful are scissors for trimming leaves, tweezers for nipping, and brushes for cleaning topsoil.

Most bonsai material is started in training pots which are larger than bonsai pots. These will hold the heavy roots, which are gradually cut back until small fibrous roots develop. All kinds of containers can be used as training pots—clay saucers, plastic containers, wooden boxes of many sizes. The pot should be large enough to accommodate the tree's root system and should be similar in shape to the bonsai pot which will eventually replace it. For example, an upright tree, the type easiest for beginners to grow and destined for a low, flat container, should be grown in a fairly low training pot. It should be placed slightly off-center in an oval or rectangular pot.

The color of the bonsai pot should contrast with the tree's foliage. Use white, tan, or green pots for trees with brightly colored flowers or fruits. Use unglazed pots with pines and deciduous trees.

Generally, bonsai containers come in five shapes—

round, oval, square, rectangular, and hexagonal. In each shape there is a wide variety of sizes. You can obtain the pots from some of the larger Chinese or Japanese hardware stores, or from department stores that offer imported items.

In the garden, display your bonsai on simple shelves, set on concrete blocks. Place the shelves against an outside wall away from trees and protect them from the sun. Bonsai in large containers look best displayed alone. Place them on some kind of stand, rather than setting them on the ground.

Indoors, bonsai look well placed in front of a plain wall on a raised stand. The Japanese display them on a platform raised a few inches above the floor in one corner of the living room. Paintings and scrolls are hung against the wall at the back. Other objects, such as ceramic ware or flower arrangements, are grouped with bonsai on the platform—but it is the cherished bonsai that have pride of place.

For Further Reading

Bonsai for Americans, by George Frederick Hull (Doubleday and Co., Inc., New York, 1964)

Bonsai for Pleasure, by Keiji Murata and Takema Takeuchi (Japan Publications, Tokyo, 1969)

Step by Step to Growing Bonsai Trees, by Jean Melville (Hippocrene Books, New York, 1973)

Bonsai with American Trees, by Masakuni Kawazumi and

Kyuzo Murata (Kodansha International, New York, 1975)

MAKING LONG-LASTING FLOWER AND FOLIAGE ARRANGEMENTS

If you have a garden, or are within reach of fields, woods, or wetlands, you have abundant material at hand for the hobby of making long-lasting "arrangements." Huge bouquets of dried material are very popular. Such an arrangement might include everlastings, silver dollars, grasses, dried flower heads, and—if you can find any—peacock feathers, which seem to "belong." The whole can be lightly sprayed with gold or bronze but looks every bit as beautiful if left with its own subtle gradation of natural colors.

You will need a warm, dry room to work in. Mrs. John Beach, of Old Tappan, New Jersey, uses her furnace room, in which she has installed a dehumidifier. "People often think that dried flowers fade in the sunlight," she says, "but they actually lose color when the moisture is not removed."

Because dried flowers shrink in size, you will need twice as much material for dried arrangements as for fresh. With the exception of iris, gladioli, and petunias, almost all garden flowers dry well. You will also need florist's wire, boxes, utensils, and containers.

There are four methods to choose from, all comparatively simple. "Some people have more of an inborn talent for arrangement," says Mrs. Beach, "but with one or two lessons and a good book, I don't see why anyone can't make flower arrangements."

According to their type, you can press your flowers, hang them in a dry room, dry them with an agent, or treat them with glycerine. When Mrs. Beach started her collection, she preserved her flowers by pressing them in a book. Now she uses one of the available flower presses, which come in sizes of 7″ or 11″ square. Best for pressing are ferns, leaves, and single flowers, which are usually dry within five days. Most of the moisture evaporates but enough is left so that the fern will curve when placed in a container.

A bunch of grasses, or half a dozen large flowers stripped of their foliage, can be hung upside down to dry in a dark, warm room. They will be ready in a week to ten days. Straw flowers are usually dried in this way.

Drying with an agent is more complicated but is worthwhile for ball-shaped flowers like roses and chrysanthemums. Excellent results can be obtained with such an agent as Natrasorb, blue crystals with which you can preserve the beauty of flowers for months. (When the crystals turn pink, simply dry them in the oven until they turn blue again and can be reused). Natrasorb is obtainable from Multiform Desiccant Products, Inc., Buffalo, New York 14213, or from a florist or hobby center.

To dry flowers with Natrasorb, you will need a supply of crystals, florist's wire, masking tape, a cookie tin, and an artist's brush. Attach a piece of medium-weight wire to the short stem of a flower. This will help to position it for drying and will make it flexible enough to be bent into artistic arrangements.

Fill the cookie tin with Natrasorb to a depth of two inches. Insert larger flowers face down and smaller ones face up. Sprinkle the crystals all over the flowers, moving them gently around so that all parts are covered.

Cover the cookie container with a tight-fitting top and seal it with masking tape. Store it undisturbed for from three to five days. Then slowly pour off the crystals, gently blowing away leftover particles. Use the artist's brush for delicate areas. Once cleaned of crystals, the flowers are ready for use in arrangements.

The glycerine method preserves foliage and keeps it pliable indefinitely. A mixture of one-third of glycerine to two-thirds of water is used. The stems of the flowers should be ten inches long, crushed about halfway up to allow for rapid absorption. Immerse the foliage in the solution until absorption takes place. This can take from three days to three weeks.

Whatever method you use, your flowers should be picked between noon and two o'clock, during their dryest period. Pick them when they are about three-quarters open, just before full bloom.

When the flower-collecting season nears its end, you can purchase dried material from florists' shops and make your own arrangements. Or take to the woods and wetlands for their bounty of pinecones and leaves.

Six-foot rushes can be used to advantage. (Cut them with a sharp knife to prevent skinning your hands.) Rushes look stunning when sprayed with gold, and a large clump will be eye-catching and will last for years.

For Further Reading

Resin and Glass Artcraft for Flower Arrangers and Craftsmen, by Lura Smith (William Morrow and Co., Inc., New York, 1966)

Decorating with Plant Crafts and Natural Material, by Phyllis Pautz (Doubleday and Co., Inc., New York, 1971)

Getting Started in Dried Flower Craft, by Barbara Amlick (The Macmillan Co., New York, 1971)

Flower Arrangements That Last, by Marian Klamkin (The Macmillan Co., New York, 1968)

Dried Flowers from Antiquity to the Present: A History and Practical Guide to Flower Drying, by Leonard Karel (Scarecrow Press, Inc., Metuchen, N.J., 1973)

CHAPTER EIGHT

Hobbies with Living Creatures

RAISING GOLDFISH

For the hobbyist who lives in an apartment where such pets as cats and dogs are not permitted, raising goldfish makes a satisfying hobby. The fish are amusing, take up little space, and are easy to feed and keep clean.

As they are likely to be with you for several years, it is worthwhile to provide your fish with the right kind of home. Take time to get it ready well in advance of buying the fish. A rectangular tank is best, and it should contain a gallon of water for each fish. The round glass bowl so often used is unsuitable and actually cruel; it causes overcrowding and suffocation. Some fish-lovers once showed their disapproval of this type by forming an association known as the Society for the Prevention of Round Goldfish Bowls.

If possible, fill your tank with rain water. Then cover the bottom with sand and plant some water plants in it. You can buy these quite cheaply at a commercial aquarium or pet store. If you have enough plants, the water will never need changing. Wait until the plants are growing nicely before you buy your fish.

You will find a variety of fish in the pet store and sometimes in the dime store. Look for healthy specimens. Those you choose should be at least 1½″ long, not including the tail, with 2″ to 3″ even better. Don't buy fish that have chewed fins, a whitish mouth, or blood on the body or fins. The common varieties with slender tails and bodies usually do better than fancier kinds with elaborate fins and tails.

The hardiest and commonest types are colored white, orange, red, black, or a mixture of these colors. These are the best to start with. Later—as all kinds of goldfish will live peacefully together—you might add something more exotic, like a graceful fantail or a lionhead, or a telescope-eyed fish.

The store will give you the fish in either a plastic bag or a bucket containing water from their tank. When you get home, place the receptacle in the water in your tank until the water inside the bag or bucket equals the temperature of the tank. This usually takes about fifteen minutes. Then, with a large net, quickly remove your new fish from the receptacle and let them swim gently into the aquarium. Some people throw them into the tank but this hurts and scares them. Incidentally, use a net whenever you have to take them out of the water; never hold them in your hand.

Feeding your fish is simple. You can buy prepared food, but they much prefer fresh food like bran, breadcrumbs, earthworms, and the insects they find on the water plants in their aquarium. If you are not squeamish, you will find it rewarding to feed them regularly with bits of earthworm. It makes the fish surprisingly tame.

When they are well treated, goldfish can live for from five to seven years. But be careful not to overfeed them; more fish die from overfeeding than from all other ailments put together. If your fish get sick, it is kinder to destroy than try to cure them—though there is one cure that sometimes makes a fish perk up. That is, put them into green water—water in which flowers have been standing. But it is best to destroy at once any fish which develop fungus (a white, cottony appearance) or parasites (white spots). These diseases are highly infectious and could kill off all your fish.

No matter how pretty goldfish may look in the sunlight, *never keep your aquarium in a sunny window.* Fish have no eyelids, so you can easily imagine the torture that sunlight would cause them. What is more, sunlight makes the water green and slimy by encouraging the growth of algae.

One last warning. Don't change the temperature of the water abruptly. Goldfish can live well at any temperature from 60 to 80 degrees, but sudden changes are injurious to them. They suffer, and sometimes die, if you move them to a tank of much colder water. So, if you change or add water to your aquarium, make sure that it is lukewarm.

Goldfish originally came from China and Japan, where they live happily in rivers. They are too delicate to live outdoors in colder climates, but can be kept in garden pools in summer, where they are likely to breed. For the impatient hobbyist with access to an outdoor pool, raising goldfish would be a good choice. An easy, inexpensive hobby, it gives quick results. Spawning usually starts in May, and the eggs, which attach themselves to water plants, hatch out in a week.

During the breeding season, the male fish will develop tubercles (small, knoblike lumps) on the gills, and the female will grow fatter. When you spot the eggs attached to the water plants, remove the plants carefully to an already prepared aquarium. This is the only sure way of hatching the eggs, because goldfish are cannibalistic and will often eat their eggs.

For your newly hatched fish you will need a supply of green water. This contains various kinds of microscopic life, which is excellent nutrition. You can also feed tiny amounts of boiled oatmeal, or yolk of egg rubbed through a sieve.

For Further Reading

Strange Breeding Habits of Aquarium Fish, by Hilda Simon (Dodd, Mead and Co., New York, 1975)

KEEPING CAGE BIRDS

For centuries, birds have been man's companions and pets, treasured for their song or beauty, or—in the case of mynah birds, parrots, and others—for their astonishing ability to talk and mimic their owners. The keeping of cage birds is a highly enjoyable hobby, especially suitable for those who cannot accommodate the larger and livelier pets. Properly cared for, your birds will live happily for years.

Until recently, only the wealthy could afford exotic birds. But today, with faster and less expensive transportation, we can import birds from all over the world. We have learned, too, to breed our own birds, even rare ones, and have "created" kinds which do not exist in the wild.

You will find birds for sale in street markets, pet shops, department-store pet centers, and breeders' establishments. The number of different kinds available is fantastically large. Your choice need only be limited by price and by the space available for housing them.

As a beginner, it is best not to buy in the street market; without special knowledge, you might come away with something that will later prove to be imperfect. Make your purchase from a well-established pet store or bird importer; with his reputation to protect, the dealer will sell you healthy birds.

Before you buy, browse around and get acquainted with everything from budgerigars—parakeets—to South American sugarbirds. Your birds will be with you for years, so take time to decide whether you want a familiar parrot, canary, or macaw, or something as exotic as a foreign goldfinch. While still a beginner, avoid the very exotic bird; the more common species will be hardier and easier to care for.

The rules for keeping your birds healthy are simple and are the same for all birds, common and exotic. Cleanliness is vital. Quarters must be kept spotlessly clean, which means a weekly scrubbing with hot water. Drinking vessels and seed containers must also be kept free of dirt.

Make sure that your cages are the right size and shape. Canaries, for instance, are best housed in a *long* cage, because they fly horizontally and a short cage restricts their exercise. Budgerigars should preferably be kept in a rather larger cage than the kind usually sold for them.

Sufficient cage or flight space is important both physically and psychologically. Boredom and monotony can be as harmful to your birds as dirt. Parrots, especially, enjoy exercise, and their cages should be fitted with a swinging perch.

Temperature must be taken into consideration. Hardier birds will be happy and comfortable in an outdoor or porch aviary at all times of year, provided they have shelter from rain, snow, and sleet. Other birds need artificial heat, even during the warmest weather.

Birdseeds suitable for the various kinds of birds can be purchased in pet stores. Budgerigars, for instance, do well on a mixture compounded of one part panicum millet to two parts of good, cleaned canary seed. Because of their size, parrots and larger birds need larger-sized food grains; these specially prepared foods are also on sale, but the bigger birds also relish an occasional tidbit in the form of fruit or greenstuff. They delight in shelled nuts, too.

To keep birds in prime condition, plenty of green food should be given when available. When there is none, a substitute may be made by sprouting some grain in warmth, moisture, and darkness. Cuttlebone and a constant supply of grits, both necessary, are obtainable in pet stores.

Twigs or small branches from trees make good temporary perches and provide the birds with something to peck and worry. Take care, however, to see that such material is nonpoisonous and that it has not been sprayed with any insecticide or herbicide.

For Further Reading

Aviary Birds, by Rosemary Low (A.S. Barnes and Co., Inc., Cranbury, N.J., 1970)

Aviary and Cage Birds: Three Books in One (Borden Publishing Co., Alhambra, Calif.)

Introducing Birds as Pets, by Howell Evans and Edmund Burke (Paul Hamlyn, Ltd., London, 1963)

PIGEON RAISING

Housed in airy lofts, pigeons provide a hobby and a sport for thousands. Pigeon raising and pigeon flying are serious business, with first-class birds fetching over a thousand dollars. Pigeon pedigrees and performance records form a vast library, and there are national and international races every year.

All our domestic pigeons are descendants of the common rock dove, known as the Blue Rock pigeon, which is indigenous to North America. In the process of domestication, pigeons have branched out into many varieties, some having been developed for utility purposes, some for their beauty.

Pigeons were first domesticated about 3000 B.C. By 1150 B.C., the Sultan of Baghdad had actually established a pigeon post. Unfortunately, it was destroyed when Baghdad fell into Mongol hands.

During the French Revolution, pigeons were widely used as messengers, and their bulletins were printed in Belgian and French newspapers. In 1849, pigeons carried telegrams part of the way between Brussels and Berlin, filling a gap in the telegraph lines.

During World War I, both sides used pigeons extensively as messengers. In World War II, they were frequently used by the secret services and partisans, especially in Yugoslavia. Aircraft of coastal commands all carried at least one pigeon to establish contact with their base should the plane be forced down and the transmitter wrecked.

Today, Belgium is considered to be the home of the pigeons. Every village, even the tiniest, has its *Société Colombophile,* or pigeon club. The annual Belgian *Concours National,* a race of about five hundred miles from

Toulouse to Brussels, was started in 1881 and set the model for races in other countries.

If you decide to make pigeon raising your hobby, you will need a commanding site for a loft—perhaps a roof, an old barn, or a lofty garden shed. You, or the local carpenter, can build the loft according to the plans provided in such a book as *How to Raise and Train Pigeons* by William H. Allen.

Part of the loft will be an aviary, usually built of wire netting open on the side and roof. Here the pigeons will get more sunlight than in the loft proper. Perches are placed on the inner sides of the loft walls, and a trap is specially constructed to allow the pigeons free passage into, but not out of, the loft. A trap that permits the pigeon to enter at will is known as an "open trap." In front of the loft is placed a landing board on which the pigeons alight when about to enter. The loft is provided with drinking fountains, bath pans, grit boxes, and other equipment for maintaining sanitary conditions.

All homing pigeons except those reserved for breeding purposes undergo training continuously from the time they are twenty-eight days old. The training consists of teaching them to enter the loft through the trap, exercising around the loft, and returning to the loft when set free at a more distant point. The pigeon's desire to return is based on its hunger or on its wish to be with its mate. As pigeons mate for life, the latter desire is often the stronger.

Adult pigeons are capable of eating their own body

weight every day, and the right diet is important. It should include leguminous seeds, cereal grains, green foods, and grit. The seeds and grains are fed as an ordinary diet in the form of a food mixture. All seeds and grains, no matter what type, must be clean, sound, and of a good natural color and odor.

Make sure that the birds have a good supply of uncontaminated drinking water. Pigeons, incidentally, do not drink in the same way as most birds; they thrust their beaks into the water and keep them there until their thirst is quenched.

Pigeons lay two or three white eggs at a time, and the squab, or female bird, feeds her young by regurgitation. The crop of the mother bird expands, and glands within it secrete a milky fluid which mixes with her half-digested food. This is then pumped back up and into the nestling, the mother bird forcing her beak down into that of the young one.

If you hope to train your pigeons for racing, you will need to ensure that they have good health and the necessary strength to endure long flights. Good health is dependent upon the sanitation of the loft, proper feeding of a suitable diet, ventilation, and uncontaminated drinking water. The strength of the bird is increased by exercise flights around the loft, and by the training flights the bird may receive from points that are distant from the loft.

Pigeon fanciers usually divide their birds into two classes, one for breeding and the other for racing, although the racing birds are sometimes allowed to breed. When entered in a race, they are shipped to a departure point in big wicker cages, holding food and water. At the start of a race, the competitors are banded with a rubber countermark and are set free by a starter who notes the time of release. The birds ascend rapidly, become oriented, and head directly for their lofts. As they enter the loft, the rubber countermark is removed and placed in a pigeon timer which indicates the time of arrival. The distance of the pigeon's flight is divided by the time consumed to determine which pigeon has made the fastest speed. A bird is not considered to have arrived "home" until it is actually through the trap of its loft.

Even when pigeons are not actually breeding or racing, they must be kept in condition. To accomplish this, the birds are flown every day, returning to the loft at the end of the exercise period.

For Further Reading

Couriers of the Sky: Pigeons and Their Care, by Mary F. Bonner (Alfred A. Knopf, Inc., New York, 1952)

How to Raise & Train Pigeons, by William H. Allen (Sterling Publishing Co., Inc., New York, 1972)

CHAPTER NINE

Treasure Hunting Hobbies

LOCATING BURIED TREASURE

If you are looking for a way of making the time fly while you are taking exercise outdoors, try today's form of treasure hunting. Amusing, unpredictable, and sometimes profitable, it requires only one piece of equipment, a metal locator. With this device you can turn up anything from a Coca-Cola can to a gold doubloon.

Metal detectors, the modern civilian form of the Army mine detector, come in a wide range of prices. You can buy one for about $36.00, but the better ones cost one hundred dollars or more. If you are handy with tools and a soldering iron, you can get a kit for from $64.00 up and put together a sophisticated detector, created "for the serious treasure hunter." Many types of detectors are advertised in such magazines as *Treasure World* and *True Treasure*. But while it is possible for enthusiasts to pay a three-figure sum for the latest ultrasensitive type of detector, most treasure is found in the first three or four inches of soil. A cheaper model is adequate for picking up these bits and pieces.

Operating the detector is simple. You set the audible alarm at the required level and slowly sweep the detector over the ground where you hope treasure is located. When the detector is above metal, it will emit a growling or buzzing sound—and, if there are people nearby, you will soon have an audience to cheer you on. "This particular kind of treasure hunting is not a game for the self-conscious," says journalist Peter Jenkins, speaking from his own experience.

Base metals like copper cause only a dull noise. Brilliant metals, and stones like diamonds, cause a high-pitched whine. (So, unfortunately, do such things as silver paper and baked-bean cans!)

Good spots for treasure hunting are everywhere. In the city, demolition sites are often a source of valuable old coins. At the seashore, especially after a holiday, there is treasure aplenty a few inches down in the sand—coins, pins, bracelets, and bits of jewelry. In La Jolla, California, a 71-year-old man prowls the beaches twice a week with his detector. He wears a hat covered with pins he has turned up in the sand—a mouse, a lobster, a Girl Scout World Friendship pin, and others. Among his finds are a whole canful of wheat sheaf pennies, fifty gold or silver rings, dozens of spoons, and coins ranging from nickels to half dollars. The pride of his collection is a diver's watch. A friend of his walks the city streets instead of the beach, trailing his detector in the gutters. He picks up an amazing number of coins each day.

Thomas Murphy of Brooklyn, New York, combines his hobbies. When he walks his dog, Skipper, each morning and evening, he watches the sidewalks and streets and finds all sorts of unusual things—an oriental necklace, a surgical instrument dropped by a doctor from a nearby hospital—and, of course, coins. Murph, as he is affectionately known, walks the sands at Coney Island every afternoon with a group of health-minded friends. He does not bother with a detector but prefers to use his eyes, invariably turning up something interesting, from a gold ring to a viewfinder.

Beneath a river bridge or in the silt on the outside bend of a river are places where there is likely to be something worth discovering. In the country, abandoned farms and old campsites are promising. Darrell and Marie Johnson, out with their new metal detector, spotted a lone fencepost near a tumbledown barn; close to it, they turned up an old Mason jar containing two crumpled fifty-dollar bills.

The real experts do some advance browsing in their history books to choose their spots. "I know some who even go down to the British Museum in London to try and discover the whereabouts of an ancient battlefield," says John Perkins.

In the United States, while using his detector around an old homesite near Baker, Louisiana, Herbert Babin dug up a British shilling, dated 1652 and worth $3,200. Louis Miller located a museum piece, a 20-pound chunk of the most famous sculpture in early American history. It is part of an equestrian statue of King George III. The statue had been mysteriously removed from its site in Bowling Green Park, in New York City, and had been broken up and dumped in a swamp in Wilton, Connecticut.

With persistence, you may, like Louis Miller, make treasure hunting pay off. Louis, who owns a tiny store where he sells antiques and junk, uses his detector to get merchandise for his shelves. Among the things he has turned up are rings, horseshoes, bronze statues, cuff links, keys, old toys, and an impressive collection of coins. One of the medals he located in the sand along Long Island Sound is a turn-of-the-century commemorative item; it shows the first flight over the English Channel made by Louis Blériot in 1909.

For Further Reading

The Electronic Metal Detector Handbook, by E. S. LeGaye
Hidden Treasure, by Charles S. Albano
Introduction to Treasure Hunting, by Alan Smith
Coin Shooting: How and Where To Do It, by Glenn Carlson
The above books available from Treasure Book Headquarters, Drawer L, Conroe, Texas, 77301
Monthly periodicals: *True Treasure* and *Treasure World*

(True Treasure Publications, Inc., Drawer L, Conroe, Texas 77301)

BARGAIN HUNTING, UNLIMITED

The many types of neighborhood sales—garage, basement, flea market, warehouse, lost property, etc.—suggest an amusing hobby for energetic people with time on their hands. If you enjoy shopping but have little excuse for browsing around, why not bargain hunt for friends and neighbors who have no time to look for a special object they need or want?

Shopping for others is an excellent idea for hobbyists who live in a small town or in, or near, a populous suburb. If you are looking for a new hobby, one with which you can make a small profit, give it a try. You'll get some not-too-strenuous exercise, meet a variety of people, and have many tales to tell of your experiences. You can pursue your hobby alone, or with a friend.

All you need to start with is a notebook and pencil, cash or your checkbook (you will get back your outlay when you deliver the goods), and a pair of stout walking shoes. It is sensible to subscribe to one or two local papers of the districts near your home; they will carry advertisements and announcements of sales in your area. Have at hand, too, a good street map of the neighborhood where you will hunt.

Begin by asking friends, relatives, neighbors, club

members if they have any special "wants." Jot down details; size, color, material, etc. Note the price they are willing to pay—and stay within it. And be wary; don't make rash promises about when you will deliver; you may be lucky enough to find the item quickly, or you may not!

When you have a list of at least six "wanted" items, start looking. Avoid regular stores, where bargains are few. Junk and secondhand stores are sometimes a source, with Salvation Army stores offering everything from bric-a-brac to clothing at very modest prices. Women's Exchanges, too, stock a wide variety of quality china, pictures, and such, but the prices are generally high. Lost property sales, held at intervals by the post office and railroads, are advertised in the local papers and are a splendid source of rainwear, umbrellas, walking sticks, and attaché cases.

Warehouse sales of offbeat items are worth visiting. Not long ago, a large department store advertised a sale of used display items in its suburban warehouse (usually a clearance center for furniture and carpets). The manager did not expect much response but thought that amateur dramatic clubs or small store owners might buy some of the items for props or window dressing. To his surprise, the store was swamped with bargain hunters. One browser found the white wagon wheel she wanted for a garden ornament. She also picked up an old doll cradle, explaining that it would appeal to a collector of antique toys who had asked her to "keep an eye out" for items for his collection.

The most amusing and fruitful sales to visit, however, are the flea markets. These abound, and are here to stay; there are over a hundred every year in Bergen County, New Jersey, alone. The best type is the outdoor market, where dealers sell items from the past and present, using crowded tables and tightly packed baskets, with boxes and cartons underneath the tables. Flea markets are a fine place to shop for the "wants" of young marrieds—things like old trunks (for decoration and storage) or old iceboxes that can be converted into bars. Do not, however, actually buy such items unless you have a customer waiting for them; if you spot something that you think may be appreciated, take a picture of it, if possible, or jot down a brief description. Then, when you locate a buyer, you can come back and get it.

If you are looking for collectors' items, watch out for *specialized* flea markets. A typical one was recently held under the auspices of the North Jersey Antique Bottle Collectors; the fifty participating dealers were required to restrict 60 per cent of their wares to bottles.

When the weather is poor, visit the indoor flea markets. Most towns have at least one, sometimes run by the local historical society. If you prefer to stay close to home, then browse in the garage, basement, and pre-moving-day sales in your neighborhood. Your local paper will carry advertisements of them, and you can get a pretty accurate idea of what you will find there. If you are searching for a single item, save yourself time by telephoning in advance to ask whether such an object is to be included in the sale.

Auction sales can be a good source of bargains—if you keep your head. Look around the auction room before the sale and decide what you want to bid on. At the sale, stand where you can see and hear—and be heard. "But don't wave your hands or make wild gestures unless you are bidding," says Ann Kilborn Cole, expert on antiques, "or you may find a horrible umbrella stand has just been knocked down to you for ten dollars!" If what you are looking for is an antique, remember that you are taking a chance by buying at auction. All sales are final, and you will have no recourse whatever in case of any dissatisfaction.

Country auctions are worth attending, if only for their amusement value. William Paul Bricker, author of books on antiques, tells of a musical powder box that was put up for sale. At the time, such boxes were seldom seen in the country and the auctioneer spun a fine story, declaring that the musical box was probably a century old. It sold for $25.00 and the buyer was sure he had acquired a treasure. Actually, the tune it played dated it; it had been composed only ten years earlier!

To shop profitably at sales of any kind, keep the following rules in mind. Do not buy on impulse; buy only what you have been asked to find. Keep your eyes wide open; look in every corner and at the very bottom of every basket and box. When you see something you are not sure about, *hold on to it* while you are considering. An unwritten law allows anyone to buy any article resting on the counter. A good piece has often been lost because the would-be purchaser put it back on the counter for a moment—where it was promptly grabbed by another buyer.

How much can you charge for your service in finding a particular object? From 10 to 15 per cent of the price is fair, depending upon the trouble you went to. Do not engage to buy anything "on approval" for your client; people sometimes change their minds and you may be left with the item. Do not engage to buy anything that is very bulky, or very expensive. Do not undertake to store or wrap objects, except in exceptional circumstances and at an extra charge.

Finally, do not take on too many commissions at a time; a dozen "wants" jotted down in your notebook are enough. Too many items to look for can cause confusion.

For Further Reading

The Garage Sale Manual, by Jim and Jean Young (Praeger Publishers, Inc., New York, 1973)

The Getting Game, by George Daniels (Harper and Row, Publishers, New York, 1974)

Fortune in the Junk Pile, by Dorothy H. Jenkins (Crown Publishers, Inc., New York, 1970)

MAKING SOMETHING OUT OF NOTHING

The most challenging contemporary hobby, one which gives huge satisfaction to the hobbyist, is making something out of nothing. Or, more accurately, out of all kinds of leftovers.

Most people can come up with plenty of material for this hobby. But those who have no overflowing attic or stuffed closets can still get all they need from local factories. At Recycle, a Boston center, you can walk away with a shopping bag crammed with factory junk. Then the fun starts. What can you make from squeezable orange cylinders, strange plastic shapes, or wooden "feet" (really molds once used in shoe factories)?

The center's overseer, Robin Simmons, runs workshops to show what can be done with such junk. She fashions marionettes out of cardboard circles, dolls out of foam rubber, weighing devices out of merchandise display tubes, and wonderful children's games from the Swiss-cheese-like sheets of plastic and rubber out of which gaskets have been punched.

By now there is a growing literature of leftovers, books which will give you suggestions for dozens of things you can make from junk. In *Art from Found Materials,* available from your library, Mary Lou Stribling tells how to turn weathered wood, tin cans, feathers, stones, fabrics, and paper into wall hangings, jewelry, decorative centerpieces, candleholders, and other attractive things.

Or you can simply keep your eye on the feature page of the newspaper. Hobbyists are being written up in a big way, and many of their ideas will spark your own imagination. If you need more information, write to the hobbyist in question; they are happy to "tell all."

Following are typical, something-out-of-nothing hobbies which you might like to adopt.

In Concord, New Hampshire, Eva S. Dean uses leftover yarn of all colors and thicknesses to make cuddly kittens of various sizes—exclusively. She has custom-made hundreds—plain, variegated, and two-toned (main color plus white paws and nose). Customers dote on these kittens and buy them for nurseries, for gifts, and for decorative purposes. One customer ordered one to wear on her coat to match her hat.

In Woburn, Massachusetts, Ira D. Clark has a unique way with empty cans. After cleaning them thoroughly, he cuts the metal into half-inch strips. These he twists into miniature rocking chairs, sofas, and footstools. He paints them black, red, silver, or gold, and finishes them off with plump velvet cushions, stuffed with foam. (If you want to know more precisely how he does it, you can get in touch with Ira at 30 Stoddard St., Woburn, Massachusetts 01801.)

William Hasse of East Haven, Connecticut, discovered something to do with that least promising of leftovers—nutshells. Three years ago, he experimented in making "nutty objects"—trivets, pictures, signs, bracelets, clips, belts, etc. Since then, his products sell at church affairs, and in flea markets and craft shows. "The best nuts to use are black walnuts, butternuts, and hickory nuts," he told an interviewer from *Yankee* magazine. "I slice them one-quarter inch thick with a metal hacksaw, varying the angle of the slice to produce different designs. Peachstones are halved or sawed lengthwise or sideways."

Anna Marie Clarie, of Nutley, New Jersey, has found amusing and beautiful ways of using all kinds of bits and pieces—driftwood, which she picks up on various beaches; dried flowers and insects; prints from greeting cards; even old eyeglass lenses. From the latter, she makes pins which are colorful miniature reproductions of classical and baroque paintings. She applies a print to the lens, glues it on, sprays it with several coats of varnish, and waxes or buffs it.

At eighty-five, Mrs. G.F. Gray of Lyndon, Vermont, collects bits of bark from felled or dead trees, or loose pieces that are ready to drop off. When the bark is completely dry, she separates it into three or four layers and cuts it into various shapes and sizes, large for pictures, smaller for Christmas and greeting cards. She wipes the surface with a damp cloth and then uses watercolors to paint her scene, allowing the bark's surface to suggest the design.

For Further Reading

Don't Throw It Away! by Vivian Abell (Creative Home Library, Meredith Corp., Des Moines, Iowa, 1973)

Dictionary of Discards, by F.M. Rich (Association Press, New York, 1952)

Tin-Can Crafting, by Sylvia Howard (Sterling Publishing Co., Inc., New York, 1964)

CHAPTER TEN

A Look at Some Offbeat Art

Where hobbies are concerned, it is often difficult to differentiate between arts and crafts. Some hobbyists combine the two. They work in such unlikely media as string, stones and sand, and the results are often more art than craft, although a mixture of the two.

STRING ART

Abstract, realistic, and free-form designs can be beautifully executed in string. Mrs. J.A. Fortier, of Waukegan, Illinois, has taught string art successfully in the public and private schools of her state. Today her son, mechanical engineer Jean Fortier, creates string pictures as his hobby. He says that figuring out the design is an interesting engineering problem. Although he began with geometrics, contriving pictures from ovals, circles, and triangles, he now prefers representational, three-dimensional forms. After hours of layout sketching and color coordination, he sets to work with cardboard, needle, and string. The end result is a charming and delicate string picture of an owl, cat, mouse, bicycle, eagle, or butterfly.

Hobbyists turning to string art will find all they need to know in *Designing Pictures with String,* by Robert E. Sharpton. It lists the inexpensive, readily available materials needed, and gives step-by-step instructions for making string pictures of many subjects. As soon as you become reasonably expert, you will find a ready market for your pictures. A good piece of string art sells from $25.00 up, and string art designs make very acceptable gifts.

For Further Reading

String Art, Step by Step, by Robert E. Sharpton (Chilton Book Co., Philadelphia, Pa., 1975)

Designing Pictures with String, by Robert E. Sharpton (Emerson Books, Inc., New York, 1974)

STONE ART

Helen Norwood, of Wolfeboro, New Hampshire, may be the only person making "pebble people"; but if you have access to a beach or quarry, there is nothing to stop you from adopting her hobby. Using stones which she chooses and matches, she makes everything from a frog small enough to nestle in a palm to a 150-pound, 2-foot-high pelican.

Mrs. Norwood's knowledge of geology is a help in her choice of stones. Lacking this knowledge, you will have to fall back on the trial method. Look for hard, basic stones, as well as for prettily shaped and colored specimens. Mrs. Norwood collects large quantities of igneous granite and peridotite, as well as marble and magnetite. Sometimes she uses sedimentary rock for an animal's head or legs. Some such book as *A Field Guide to Rocks and Minerals,* by Frederick H. Pough, obtainable at your local library, will help you to identify the rocks you find.

After she has assembled all the needed body parts (which should be stones of the same color or grain), Mrs. Norwood tapes them together. For joining one rock to another, and for "fill-ins" (necks, muscles, ears, etc.), she chooses a heavy-duty, industrial, epoxy-type adhesive. For eyes and noses, she selects gleaming, semi-precious stones, such as obsidian, amethyst, or goldstone.

PAINTING IN A BOTTLE

Although she started her novel hobby for her own pleasure, Marion Roop, of Nantucket Island, Massachusetts, finds that she has a ready market for her art. She paints New England scenes (lighthouses and covered bridges are favorites) inside bottles of varying sizes and shapes.

As yet, Mrs. Roop has not published anything about how her effects are achieved, but she is willing to share her secrets. "I will be happy to answer any questions concerning my work," she told an interviewer for *Yankee* magazine, "and those persons who are interested may write to me at 9 Eagle Lane, Nantucket, Massachusetts 02554."

SAND PAINTING

An ancient art of desert-dwellers, sand painting consists of creating scenes and figures with colored sands. In the United States, the Navaho Indians learned the art from the Pueblos, who made simple drawings with corn meal. Sand painting is rare throughout the world; only in Australia and the Orient do we find other traces of this curious art.

It is not an art for the impatient or the clumsy-fingered. Sand paintings must be done without a single mistake. When Navahos copy sand-painting designs in their blankets, they deliberately make one mistake because they believe it ill-fated to reproduce a sand painting in its original form.

Early sand paintings are always flat; the artist worked on the ground. But the modern sand painter likes to make three-dimensional pictures. The sand is poured into a clear square or rectangular container, one layer at a time, and then poked with a rod or stick to create scenes or figures.

The materials for sand painting are inexpensive and are available at craft and department stores. You can buy variously colored sands in 12-ounce bags and assemble the simple tools yourself, but it is simpler to invest in a kit. A beginner's kit contains three packages of sand, a spoon, a pointed wooden tool, and a clearly illustrated instruction booklet. More expensive kits include clear plastic tumblers, or 4-inch-high transparent flowerpots.

Philip Perl, who is currently working on a book about sand painting, recently published some how-to notes in *The New York Times.* "You can make a mountain by spooning brown sand gently against the front of the container," he suggests. "To put snow on the mountain, poke a slight depression in the top and fill with white sand, pressing the white sand into the mountain with short, swift strokes of a knitting needle against the front of the container. This will give the effect of jagged, icy peaks."

Abstract designs are the easiest to make. You can create one by pouring a few layers of sand, in different, harmonizing colors, into the container, and then poking firmly through the top layer to the layers below while turning the container slowly around.

Cacti or ferns and figurines combine well with sand paintings. If you are going to use them, finish your design about two-thirds of the way up from the bottom, to leave space for soil for the plants. Water sparingly, and keep cacti in the sun and ferns in the shade.

For your reading pleasure (no instructions for sand painting are given), there is an enlightening chapter on this art in *Adventures in Making: Romance of Crafts Around the World,* by Seon Manley.

MINIATURE ART

For those who have a love of precision and who thrive on a challenge, miniature art is an appealing hobby. Because of their novelty, well-executed miniatures find ready buyers. But the art is demanding; it requires patience, excellent eyesight, love and enthusiasm for the miniature, and perseverance.

The equipment needed differs from that used by the conventional artist. The canvases range from 1″ x 2″ to 10″ x 10″. The average and by far the favorite size is 4″ x 5″. To be a genuine miniature, the subject must be represented no larger than one-sixth of its actual size.

The brushes used are of sable, ranging in size from No. 00 to Nos. 4 and 5. The miniatures can be created in watercolors, acrylics, and mixed media, as well as in the traditional oils.

The most essential tool is a magnifying glass. Various sizes are obtainable, and the choice is a matter of preference. Many hobbyists like to use the loupe glass, which can be fitted into the eyesocket, attached to spectacles, held in the hand, or strapped around the artist's head.

You may also use a magnifying glass on a small table-stand. The canvas is placed behind the stand, which is usually lighted.

Another kind of glass comes with clamps, which can be fixed to a miniature easel. The easel has flexible arms, which permit the glass to be set in position at any angle.

In spite of its tedious nature, miniature painting has many devotees. New Jersey is one of the few states which boasts an official society for painters of miniatures. It has more than one hundred members, all of whom firmly believe that the smaller the work, the more perfect the skill must be.

For Further Reading

A Book of Miniatures, by Dino Formaggio (Tudor Publishing Co., New York, 1962)

The British Miniature, by Raymond Lister (Isaac Pitman and Sons, Ltd., London, 1951)

CAMEO MAKING

An art in which Italy has long taken the lead, the making of cameos dates back to the days of the Greek sculptor Praxiteles. The hard and precious stones then used were brought from the East, and most of them were of magnificent size and color. They were carved in relief, in direct contrast to the intaglio, a gem in which the engraved subject is hollowed out, as in a seal.

One of the most famous, the Gonzaga, owned by the Empress Josephine and later preserved in Leningrad, represented the portraits of Nero and Agrippina.

The modern cameo cutters of Italy and elsewhere had difficulty both in locating enough fine gems and in working with them. So they introduced shell cameos. The shells of various mollusks are now used, and they are also imitated in glass.

You can carve pink and brown cameos from conch shells, or from other species whose walls have layers of different colors. If you examine a conch shell closely, you will find many small mounds of white mineral deposits in contrast to the pink background. The hobbyist chooses the spots that have the deepest deposits and cuts these sections out of the shell, using a jeweler's saw. The part that has the heaviest white is used for the head or design of the cameo.

The decoration is made by drawing an outline of the figure and then scraping away the white deposit from around the edges of the shell. This brings the design up in relief against the colored background. In earlier times, this work was done with gouges and files; today, electric drills make the process simpler.

Incidentally, the traditional cameo head (a woman with an ancient coiffure) is not the only decoration used in Italy. The designs may show profiles of people or animals. The hobbyist can also experiment with depicting a miniature landscape.

FOR FURTHER READING

For cameo cutting:

Sulphides: The Art of Cameo Incrustation, by Paul Jokelson (Thomas Nelson, Inc., New York, 1968)

CHAPTER ELEVEN

A Sampling of Crafts

Although this book presents a good number of hobbies in what might be called "arts and crafts," it can by no means exhaust all the possibilities. Not only are dozens of old crafts being revived, updated, and given a touch of sophistication, but others are constantly being invented. There seems no end to the ingenuity of the hobbyist who wants to do something "new and different."

Some of these hobbies verge on the zany. In West Orange, New Jersey, Cindy Eber decorates casts. So far as she knows, she is the first paid cast decorator in history. If you are a hospital visitor, you may like to try Cindy's hobby. Young patients, especially, appreciate having their casts brightened. Cindy's first client, a nine-year-old boy with a broken leg, wanted football players and helmets on his cast, and she supplied them. She gets from $3.00 to $15.00 for her work, depending upon the size of the cast and the complexity of the design.

Another attention-getting hobby is painting hydrants. Environmentalists in several states have painted the hydrants in their towns with whimsical designs. If you enjoy wielding a paintbrush outdoors, you might consider giving your neighborhood hydrants a rainbow charm—but check with the fire department first to make sure of its approval.

Some hobbyists, like Mrs. Lee Welliver, of Piscataway, New Jersey, like the challenge of unpromising materials. Employed by a ceramic wall and floor tile manufacturer, Mrs. Welliver is undaunted by the stony quality of the tile. She first made decorative objects out of the tiles by gluing artificial flower posies, ribbon flags, or rope-framed miniature ships on them. The results, although effective, did not satisfy her. Today she "sculpts" the tiles, producing free-standing objects, one a gleaming lighthouse which she has electrified.

She first draws an outline on the back of the tile with a glass cutter. Next she shapes it with nippers and smooths the "sculpted" result with pumice stone. If you are not afraid of a really demanding craft (". . . it takes a lot of energy," Mrs. Welliver told interviewer Shirley Friedman), you can come up with some unusual sculptures, unlikely to be duplicated anywhere.

Deciding which material you are best fitted to work with is an excellent way of choosing a hobby from among the more conventional crafts. Today's hobbies involve a wide range of media—paper, wood, leather, plastic, clay, reeds, feathers, straw, etc. Some call for such out-of-the-way materials as hoofs, horn, or bone. Following is a sampling of crafts currently in favor. When available, books giving detailed instructions for the craft are listed.

For Further Reading

Handmade: Vanishing Cultures of Europe and the Near East, by Drew and Louise Langsner (Crown Publishers, Inc., New York, 1974)

METALCRAFT

If you have had experience in working with metals, you are off to a good start. Preston Abernathy, of Haddonfield, New Jersey, is a retired tool and die maker who now devotes himself to what he calls "planar sculpture." Using brush and adhesive, he "strokes" a design or picture onto a sheet of industrial steel, a material which has always fascinated him. His pictures, with their arresting contemporary look, sell as soon as he finishes them.

This brand-new craft takes time, and exemplary patience. Mr. Abernathy buys industrial steel sheets and has them professionally buffed. First he cuts down the sheet to the size he needs and covers the metal with a special clear tape. He then inks on his design.

Using a mechanical drawing knife, he cuts away a

section of the tape and rubs the steel with a scrub brush, covered with an abrasive compound. This gives it a dull, Florentine finish. He repeats the process, bit by bit, until his design or picture is complete. Then he strips off the remaining tape and gives the steel picture a bath with a mild cleaning solution.

While Preston Abernathy has developed something new, Lawrence R. Silverstein has adopted as his hobby an art which dates back to the Greeks and Romans. He is one of the very few hobbyists who are reviving the tooled metal work known as "repoussé." Named from the French *repoussé,* meaning "from the reverse," the craft consists of creating a design in metal by beating it on the reverse side.

Mr. Silverstein draws his design first, making dozens of sketches before he is satisfied. Then, using a thick pencil, he transfers it, freehand, to a sheet of heavy, 36-gauge aluminum foil. Using a variety of woodworking tools, he begins a back-and-forth process, stretching the foil from the back, and flattening it out from the front to create raised areas. He then fills in the back depressions with Spackle, which is left to dry for three or four days. Finally, the completed work, always one-of-a-kind, is mounted on plywood or pine.

TINCRAFT

Of the metals used in crafts, tin is the least expensive and the simplest to handle. It is easy to cut and can even be bent into accordion-like pleats. Few tools are required—a pair of curved tin shears, a pair of pliers, a set of files, and some wooden molds. If you intend to make articles in which parts have to be joined with soft solder, it will be worth investing in a soldering iron.

You can make many kinds of attractive objects, whose primitive quality makes them even more appealing than brass or copper. In his cellar workshop in Plymouth, Maine, Norman Holmes coaxes out handsome copies of antique pitchers, lanterns, candleholders, boxes, and other things.

Begin by cleaning the surface of the tin thoroughly with steel wool. Then paint on the motifs, using the kind of lacquer sold for painting metal. The colors are bright but seem to "belong" to tin and have a pleasing contemporary look. Leave the background in the natural tin color.

Large items, like platters and trays, will need to be reinforced with a wooden rim or base. They are usually decorated with metal background stamps, or by using chasing tools.

For Further Reading

Tin-Can Crafting, by Sylvia Howard (Sterling Publishing Co., Inc., New York, 1959)

Top Popping, by Kenneth Patton (Chilton Book Co., Philadelphia, Pa., 1975)

WORKING WITH GLASS

Making things with glass can be as simple as bottle cutting or as complex as making objects from stained or leaded glass. Bottle cutting is currently the most popular hobby because it makes use of throwaways and reduces the local junk pile. A glass cutter and a piece of sandpaper are about all that are required to make wind chimes, drinking glasses, planters, and other attractive items.

For a more sophisticated hobby, you might like fused glass sculpture. Courses in this craft are given in many adult schools and in craft centers. Dotty and Howard Leichter, of Warren Township, New Jersey, began as ceramicists but are even more enthusiastic about fused glass. Dotty uses a spur-of-the-moment approach, but Howard plans so carefully that he can duplicate any piece he makes. For the past six years, the pair have been producing figurines of butterflies, dogs, owls, birds, and such from recycled bottles and window glass. The tiny figurines are sometimes used as jewelry items. The larger are often combined with wood or metal.

The Leichters first make a detailed sketch. They then cut out the pieces with a glass cutter, and assemble them. The sections are next glued together and glazed. Color is added before the object is put into the kiln. "I feel a little like a mad chemist as I mix colors with mortar and pestle in the studio," says Dotty.

It takes five hours to fuse a piece in the kiln. "It has

to be a slow-firing process at 1,350 degrees Fahrenheit, so as not to shatter the glass," Howard explains. The sculpture is cooled for twenty-four hours—and the waiting period is hard to bear. "There is much excitement when we lift the lid of the kiln, because we never know what the piece is going to turn out like."

For Further Reading

One Hundred and One Projects for Bottle Cutters, by Walter J. Fischman (Thomas Y. Crowell Co., New York, 1974)

MAKING STAINED GLASS

Although it takes considerable skill, even a beginner can make a variety of stained-glass objects by using the excellent kits and accessories currently on the market. The really experienced craftsman can even duplicate the famous Tiffany Tulip Lamp, a signed piece in fabulous colors which cannot be bought today for under $2,000.

Stained glass has been in use since the tenth century. The earliest known is a window in the abbey of Tegernsee, in southeast Bavaria. Early stained-glass windows consisted of a mosaic-like arrangement of pieces, the glass being stained the whole way through. Later, pictorial subjects were introduced, the roughly cut pieces of glass being set in leads and fastened to an iron tracery. Slight shadings and details were painted on the glass in *grisaille,* monochromatic painting in shades of gray.

Although other techniques were tried, the nineteenth century went back to the older method of making stained glass, and Edward Burne-Jones and William Morris designed many beautiful windows. A society of stained-glass-window enthusiasts has done much to improve and maintain modern standards of work.

Strictly speaking, "stained" glass is glass, colored or plain, upon which designs or pictures have been painted. The glass is heated in a kiln until the special paint is fused in and becomes part of the glass. The separate pieces are then assembled and "leaded" together to form the stained-glass window. "Leaded" glass is glass, colored or clear, which is bound together with lead "cames" (slender, grooved bars). Stained glass is usually leaded.

Today, most stained-glass windows are installed in churches, although different uses for the glass have emerged in New England during the past ten years. Carl Paulson, a master craftsman who left a large stained-glass company about forty years ago, now works by himself and trains apprentices in his shop, The Raven, in Upton, Massachusetts. "I make my living creating stained-glass windows for churches," he says, "but I also create decorative pieces for people who enjoy the beauty of stained glass and its potential as an art form." Mr. Paulson fashions exquisite butterflies and other ornaments which can be hung in windows to catch the sunlight.

Until he is fairly expert, the hobbyist would be well advised to begin with a kit. The Whittemore-Durgin Glass Company, of Hanover, Massachusetts, which sells every type of material, pattern, and accessory for making objects in stained or leaded glass, has a tempting range of kits to make planters, lampshades, lanterns, glass ornaments, etc. Each kit contains all you need to make the object, except solder and soldering iron. From the same firm, along with the catalog of supplies, you can get an excellent how-to leaflet, *Getting Started in Stained Glass,* for fifty cents. In text and diagrams, it explains the techniques of cutting glass, glazing, soldering, and cementing.

For Further Reading

Stained Glass Craft, by J.A. Divine and D. Blachford (Dover Publications, Inc., New York, 1972)

Glass Works: The Copper Foil Technique of Stained Glass, by Jennie French (Van Nostrand Reinhold Co., New York, 1974)

Index

NORAH SMARIDGE is the daughter of a sea captain and comes from a long line of English seafolk. After taking an Honors degree at London University, she came to New York City with her family and took writing courses at Columbia University and Hunter College.

Now writing full time, Miss Smaridge is at her desk from nine to three, and she says that it is work—but she loves it! She is the author of adult, teen-age, and juvenile fiction; biography; and light verse. She contributes articles on leisure hours to *Modern Maturity*, *Mature Years*, *N.R.T.A. Journal*, and other magazines, as well as *The New York Times*.